FREE VERSE EDITIONS

Edited by Jon Thompson

INSTANCES

JEONGRYE CHOI

SELECTED POEMS

Translated by
Brenda Hillman, Wayne de Fremery, Jeongrye Choi

PARLOR PRESS

Anderson, South Carolina | www.parlorpress.com

Parlor Press LLC, Anderson, South Carolina

© 2011 by Parlor Press
All rights reserved.
Printed in the United States of America
S A N: 2 5 4 - 8 8 7 9

Library of Congress Cataloging-in-
Publication Data

Choi, Jeongrye, 1955-
 [Poems. English]
 Instances : selected poems / Jeongrye Choi
; Translated by Brenda Hillman, Wayne de
Fremery, Jeongrye Choi.
     p. cm. -- (Free Verse editions)
 Includes bibliographical references.
 ISBN 978-1-60235-234-6 (pbk. : alk. paper)
-- ISBN 978-1-60235-235-3 (adobe ebook)
 I. Hillman, Brenda. II. Fremery, Wayne de.
III. Title.
 PR9520.9.C55A2 2011
 895.7'15--dc23
                        2011033536

Parlor Press, LLC is an independent
publisher of scholarly and trade titles in
print and multimedia formats. This book is
available in paper and Adobe eBook formats
from Parlor Press on the World Wide Web
at http://www.parlorpress.com or through
online and brick-and-mortar bookstores.
For submission information or to find out
about Parlor Press publications, write to
Parlor Press, 3015 Brackenberry Drive,
Anderson, South Carolina, 29621, or e-mail
editor@parlorpress.com.

Cover design by David Blakesley.
Interior design by Byungwook Ryu.
Cover image: "Fabulous Flowers" © 2011 by
aromanta. Used by permission.
Instances is published under the support of
the Korea Literature Translation Institute

Printed on acid-free paper.

CONTENTS

PREFATORY NOTE

It is a great pleasure to help bring Jeongrye Choi's work into an English edition. This is not the first time her writing has appeared in English, but it is the first full-length collection of her work to appear in the United States. I met the author at the University of Iowa in 2006, when she was doing a three-month residency at the International Writers' Workshop. A shy and intense person, Jeongrye was working with a couple of gifted and willing graduate students in the Writers' Workshop—Melissa Dickey and Jordan Stempleman— as well as Ryu Heewon, an exchange student from Korea studying in Iowa, and Choi Jongyoll, now an instructor of English literature in Korea. I am grateful to these writers for the work they did in rendering these versions while the author was in residence at the International Workshop, and of course to Chris Merrill for the program there.

In the middle of the semester, Jeongrye asked me if I'd be willing to help do some poems as well; I was not able to help her much when I was in Iowa, but soon learned that she would be doing a year-long residency the following year at U.C. Berkeley. We were both in touch with our friend Wayne de Fremery, an American PhD candidate in Korean Studies at Harvard, who currently lives in Seoul. Wayne knew Jeongrye's work and its place in contemporary Korean writing; since Jeongrye was just in the process of learning English and I have no Korean, Wayne agreed to provide translations.

Thus the current project began; Wayne produced the first adept versions over the next few years, and I tried to render them into English poetry. He and I spoke frequently on the phone long-distance, and Jeongrye and I met often during the year of her residency to piece together the work. We frequently sat over tea in Berkeley cafes or in my home, discussing nuances of language and of her many images in the original. Jeongrye was taking classes in English during the year. I wish I had years in my lifetime to learn the beautiful Korean language—I was completely dependent on Wayne and on Jeongrye herself.

My husband Robert Hass, who has a good knowledge of Korean poetry, describes Choi's literary background:

> Born in 1955 in Hwasŏng, Kyŏnggi Province, in the Republic of Korea, Choi belongs to the explosive generation of poets who came of age after the thirty-five-year Japanese occupation of her country, after the Korean War, and during the long struggle to rebuild South Korea's shattered economy and to transform its military dictatorships into a democratic government. These poets, not raised on Chinese classicism or Japanese poetry, were charged with the task of making a vital, modern Korean poetry. Educated in Korean poetry at Korea University, Choi has been in the middle of that generation, and, finding her way among its strands of feminist, populist, politically committed, aesthetic-minded, traditionalist, and avant-garde poetries, she has insisted on a poetry of radical freedom which she understood to be the freedom of her own mind.

There is a quality of imagination in her work that is still a rare thing in poetry—despite the opening up of form, content, and linguistic exploration that current innovative poetry has given us in the last few decades. Choi uses the image less for description than as enactment—almost as if the residue of the phantom in the poet's brain were an action in itself—of reality. And the remark is often made—among those who have attemped translation—that what translates best in poetry is the visual image or the philosophical statement. In fact, a poetic image hovers between the irrational and literal, and the great sweep of the imaginative visual realm brings in all other parts of our experience; what Pound calls phanopoeia is not simply referencing the way metaphor carries meaning but the way the eye carries both the dream and the other functions of life, as dreamtime and work-time are able to coexist in each moment. And though the best poetry brings engagement through phanopoeia, logopoeia, and melopoeia, it is often most challenging to convey syntax, rhythm, and word-sense from original languages—and thus we are lucky if the poetry is intensely visual so that the translator (or renderer, in my case) may rely on those translatable elements.

Choi's images are what might be termed "surreal," but they are also "magical realism," and at times quite abstract. At times her poetry reminds me of Barbara Guest's writing. Her style of image-making has odd wit and sweep; she makes the memory a layered reality that speaks to the current poetic moment. Her reality is a braid of metaphor, memory, intellect, and feeling. The project of trying to get Choi's work into English has been a realization about this power of the image that continues to be one of the main reasons people read poetry. Images can be quite radical—and the dazzle of Jeongrye's work can remind American readers about the mental variety and hopes for art brought from Modernism. Wayne has indicated she uses a lot of verbal play, syntactic doubling, and punning. The particular oddness of the way she sees the world is very appealing, however intense and tragic the subject matter can sometimes be. Her work is feminist in a way that I find instructive.

It has been a deep pleasure to work with Wayne de Fremery. A delightful, brilliant person with a wry sense of humor, Wayne has a vivid and dynamic relationship to both languages and has done much of the work, talking to Choi about getting the work straight into English lines and then putting them into stanzaic form; Jeongrye's English has improved over these few years, but we have been completely dependent on Wayne to get his first versions of the poems before the final versions could be made. Wayne and I are extremely grateful to LTI Korea for their financial support of the project, as well as for their many helpful suggestions in making the versions final; to poet Gillian Hamel, who advised us and helped to produce the manuscript; to Byungwook Ryu, designer, and to Jon Thompson at Free Verse Editions and Dave Blakesley at Parlor Press for their continuing belief in this work.

Everyone involved in this project is a bit of a perfectionist, and doubtless the poems might have appeared sooner, and in other words, had we not been convinced that we could do better and tried one more time. If, as Auden remarked, "poems are not finished, they are abandoned," this is doubly true of translating poems... One feels the gap, the yearning, between the first language and the alternative language, with the strokes of the signs reaching to each other—in the case of this bilingual edition, literally across the gutter of the page. Meaning is restless and cannot be trapped; it goes back and forth. I hope readers of English will find something to cherish in this work as much as I do.

Brenda Hillman

SELECTED POEMS

MOTES

We arrived, passing through that dust,
passing through that worm;
we arrived, after passing endlessly through.

I let the baby down off my back and,
while I ordered and ate *sundubu*,
and sniffled and wiped my nose,
the baby cooed
and crawled on the floor.

My age and yours—
I can't count the ages
that began in that dust.
Stone monuments have crumbled.
A lot of treasure has been buried,
even the crows have composed a long lineage.

The dust that clings to dark clothes—
little pale things holding on so stubbornly,

what do you want to be?
A cell,
a worm—
whisked off and rising up—
do you want to be a beast?

Hey, dust
clinging to dark clothes—
hey, abyss.

보푸라기들

저 티끌을 지나서 왔구나
저 벌레를 지나서
한없이 지나서 왔구나

업은 아이를 내려놓고
순두부를 시켜 먹는 동안
훌쩍거리며 코를 훔치는 동안
아이는 낄낄거리며
바닥을 기어 다니고

너의 나이 나의 나이
저 티끌에서부터의
나이를 셀 수가 없구나
그 동안 돌비는 깨어지고
많은 은금보화는 땅에 묻히고
까마귀도 긴 족보를 이루었는데*
검은 옷에 끈질기게 따라온 먼지들
악착같이 따라 붙는 희끄무레한 것들

무엇이 되고 싶은 것이냐
세포가 되었다가
버러지가 되었다가
떨치고 일어나
짐승이 되고 싶은 것이냐

검은 옷에 악착같이 따라다니는
보푸라기야
구렁텅이야

* 백석의 시 〈北方에서〉 인용

WATCHING DEER

As soon as the words were spoken,
antlers budded from his head
like branches.
As soon as the words were spoken, lights were lit and buds sprouted
behind his ears.
Somewhere, a bell rang
and the two arms thrusting forward became front legs.
Clouds descended,
dappling his back and flanks,
his belly, with spots.

Like a miracle from far away,
a baby, shaking a rattle in its stroller,
shouted something in my direction,
but I couldn't understand the words flying off.

Why was I standing here?
What were those words?

사슴 구경

그 말이 끝나자
머리에선 뿔이 돋았다
나뭇가지처럼
그 말이 끝나자 귀 뒤에서
불이 켜지고 싹이 돋았다
어디선가 종이 울리고
두 손이 엎드려 앞다리가 되었다
구름들이 내려와
등판에 배에 옆구리에
얼룩덜룩 들러붙었다

아주 멀리서 온 기적처럼
유모차에 아이가 딸랑이를 흔들며
이쪽을 향해 무어라 소리치는데
날아가던 그 말 알 수 없었다

나는 왜 여기 서 있었는지
그 말 무엇이었는지

IN THREE MINUTES

What can't we finish in three minutes?
You can have a shotgun wedding
and have a baby.
A bridge can collapse
and a department store can crumble.
A nation can be brought about.

But,
hey—
socks, pants and coats
hung out on a dusty veranda,
getting dry while you're still folded—
hey, shame and oblivion,
what are you doing?

Look at that!
A flying stone
with its wings spreading quickly
from its armpits.

Before those wings fold back up
you have to get married
and give birth,
stamp your official seal,
ask for a handshake,
start a nation.

Before the airplane crashes
and the river is dammed,
before the sand piles up on your table
and you wake the cockroach beneath your cupboard,
you should attach the green wings
under your arms.

3분 동안

3분 동안 못할 일이 뭐야
기습결혼을 하고
아이를 낳을 수 있지
다리가 끊어지고
백화점이 무너지고
한 나라를 이룰 수도 있지

그런데
이봐
먼지 낀 베란다에 널린
양말들, 바지와 잠바들
접힌 채 말라가는
수치와 망각들
뭐하는 거야

저것 봐
날아가는 돌
겨드랑이에서
재빨리 펼쳐드는 날개를

저 날개 접히기 전에
어서 결혼을 하고
아이를 낳아야지
도장을 찍고
악수를 청하고
한 나라를 이루어야지

비행기가 떨어지고
강물이 갇히기 전에
식탁 위에 모래가 켜로 앉기 전에
찬장 밑에 잠든 바퀴벌레도 깨워야지
서둘러 겨드랑이에
새파란 날개를 달아야지

BARBED WIRE IN A STREAM

We are river water flowing for the objects of our love.

Or so it seemed yesterday,
but not today.

A little breeze blew,
and leaves on a branch—each
looking a different direction,
each dancing a different dance.

Gasps in calamity
in the sky beyond, and then the clouds flow away too,
quietly coming to their senses, it would seem.

In the air, it would seem, some kind of metaphysical harvest.

냇물에 철조망

우리 모두는 사랑하는 이를 향하여 흐르는 강물이다

어제는 그렇다고 생각했는데
오늘은 아닌 것 같다

조금 바람이 불었는데
한 가지에 나뭇잎, 잎이
서로 다른 곳을 보며 다른 춤을 추고 있다

저 너머 하늘에
재난 속에서 허덕이다가 조용히 정신을 차린 것 같은 모습으로
구름도 흘러가고 있다

공중에서 무슨 형이상학적 추수를 하는 것 같다

A THIEF CAUGHT AT DUSK

All that we owned
was a shiny brass basin
and my father's pair of black shoes.

A young man in dyed fatigues
was dragged before us in handcuffs;
he hung his head.

The officer pressed:
—This one, right?
You stole it from this house. Right?

The dark of the boy's thick black eyebrows
comes back years later,
suddenly,
pressing in pursuit
at my dim evening door.

I spilled all the bright days
and this evening is lost
like a blind alley.
Yes, yes,
I just nod.

Could I really give that shining brass basin
and my father's black shoes
to the guy with a dark jacket, the dusk?

저녁에 잡혀온 도둑

그때 우리집 전 재산은
잘 닦은 놋대야와
아버지의 검은 구두 한 켤레

군복을 염색해 입은
청년이 수갑이 채워진 채 끌려와
고개를 수그리고 있었다

순경이 다그쳤다
―이 집이지?
―바로 여기서 훔쳤지?

그의 짙은 검은 눈썹같은 어둠이
수 십년이 지난 지금
갑자기
저문 내 저녁 문 앞에
몰려와 다그친다

나는 밝은 날 다 흘려 버리고
막다른 골목같은 저녁이
막막해서
그저 네 네
고개를 끄덕인다

정말 나는
검은 잠바를 입고 온 그, 저녁에게
빛나는 놋대야와 검은 구두 한 켤레를
내어줄 수나 있는 것인지

JUST A GLIMMER

In the dream,
the entrance couldn't be found.
Outside the window, one leaf shaking.
For a moment, there was a glimmering.

A peony was stuck in familiar wallpaper.
Honeysuckle stems bending
and bending;

I went to see a room for rent
and followed the guy who shuffled out in his slippers—
that was it.

Like a goldfish in a glass bowl,
I drifted for a minute, killing time,

and there I lived for decades, they say,
with one who was not my husband nor my father,
nor my son,

but someone
waving like the leaf
outside my window—
just a glimmering.

잠깐 반짝였는데

꿈엔
입구를 찾을 수 없었다
창밖에서 이파리 하나가 흔들리듯
잠깐 반짝이고 있었다

낯익은 벽지 위엔 모란이 박혀 있었다
인동초 잎덩굴은 연속해서 꼬부라지고
꼬부라지고

방을 보러 간다고 가서
슬리퍼 끌고 나온 그를 따라
들어섰을 뿐인데

유리 어항에 금붕어가 살랑이듯
잠깐 서성였는데

수십 년을 거기서 살았다고 한다
남편도 아니고 아버지도 아니고
아들도 아니었을 그와

창밖에서 이파리처럼
누군가
손을 흔들고 있었는데
잠깐 반짝였는데

"THE AIRPLANE TOOK OFF.
THE AIRPLANE DISAPPEARED."

An airplane took off.
It became a small speck and disappeared.

On Thursday, I didn't sleep at all.
On Friday, I slept all day.
Saturday and Sunday disappeared.

When I was thirty, I stood in a subway station with a baby tied to my back.
I bought a cheap camera and paid on the installment plan.
When I was twenty, I cried at a bar called the Red Ox.
I breathed charcoal gas and was hospitalized.

Another plane took off, it got rid of this place,
leaving a thin wavy line—

only he who loves, flies.
But who loves that intensely?
a poem began,
but whose? Whose poem?

He told me to get out and slammed the door behind me.
That was the first time I'd been there, but I didn't know where—
I fumbled aimlessly down a dark alley;
a plane flew noiselessly through a cloud.

비행기 떴다 비행기 사라졌다

비행기 떴다
아주 작은 점이 되어 사라졌다

목요일은 한잠도 못잤다
금요일은 하루 종일 잤다
토요일은 일요일은 사라졌다

서른살 땐 애 업고 전철역에 서 있었다
15만원 짜리 카메라를 사서 할부금을 붓고 있었다
스무살 땐 레드옥스란 술집에서 울었다
연탄가스 먹고 실려갔다

비행기가 또 떴다 이곳을 뿌리치고
가느다란 흰 선을 남기고

사랑하는 자만이 날 수 있다
그렇지만 누가 그토록 사랑하는가?
라고 시작되는 시가 있었다
누구였던가 누구의 시였던가

그는 나가라며 등 뒤에서 문을 꽝 닫았다
그 때 그곳은 처음 가본 곳이라서 어디가 어디인지
무작정 어두운 골목을 더듬어 내려오는데
비행기가 소리없이 구름 속으로 지고 있었다

The phone rang and then stopped.
This flesh is a prison; I ate sweet cream cake
and my body swelled.
I swelled behind its bars.

A truck drove along carrying a mirror:
houses piled high swayed back and forth;
an alley was swept aside, and in a moment every trace was gone.

It was a poem by Miguel Hernández.
You will not fly. You cannot fly.
However hard you struggle to take flight
you are cast away.

The plane, a heavy lump of steel, takes off recklessly,
becoming a metal island circling in the sky.

전화가 오고 전화가 끊어지고
육체는 감옥이라서 달디단 크림케익을 먹고
몸은 부풀었다
육체의 창살 안에서 부풀었다

트럭이 거울을 싣고 가고 있었다
거울 속에 집들은 통째로 실려가다 기우뚱
골목을 제끼고 순간에 자취를 감추었다

미겔 에르난데스의 시였다
너는 날 수 없으리라 너는 날 수 없다
네가 아무리 기를 쓰고 올라가도
너는 조난당하고 말리라

비행기가 무거운 쇳덩어리가 무작정 떴다
하늘 가운데 금속의 섬이 되어 돌고 있다

THE FIVE-THOUSAND-YEAR-OLD HEART
I'VE SWALLOWED

The hooves, the hooves of horses came toward me.
I stared at the ceiling bulb; I stared at the filament in the bulb, at the
little hooves.

No, I didn't know that they had come clop-clopping into my eyes from
an evening five-hundred—some five-thousand—years ago.

Why did my body miss the desert for such a long time? Why did I
borrow the body of that dying water bird to wander the empty sky?

The heart some five-thousand years old that I've swallowed listens to
the sounds of the desert's sand storm. It watches a deep-blue lake float,
rippling gently.

When morning comes I hear the shrieks of the horses that came
toward me all night as the hobnails are struck at heaven's village
blacksmith.

Do earthly flowers bloom and fall in thirst for every useless thing
in the world?

I should go on my way but it's too far; my eyes still endlessly swallow
the horses' hooves. Do the flowers bloom and fall and bloom and fall
without knowing the endless loneliness
of my bare feet?

한 오천 살은 먹은 내 마음이

말 발굽, 말 발굽이 내게로 왔다
천정의 백열등을 바라보다가 백열등 속 필라멘트, 작은 말발굽을 바라보다가

아니 오백 년 오천 년 전의 어느 저녁부터 말 발굽들이 내 눈 속으로 자그락
자그락 걸어 들어 온 것을 내가 모른 것이다

왜 내 몸이 그렇게 오랫동안 사막을 그렸는지 죽을 물새의 몸을 빌어 허공을
헤매었는지

한 오천 살은 먹은 내 마음이 사막의 모래폭풍 소리를 듣는다 짙푸른 호수가
넘실넘실 파도 치며 떠 있음을 본다

새벽이면 밤새 내게로 온 말들이 하늘마을 대장간에서 발굽에 징을 박으며
울부짖는 소리를 듣는다

세상의 모든 헛된 것에 대한 갈증으로 지상의 꽃들은 피고 지는 것일까

갈 길 멀어 아직도 내 눈은 끝도 없이 말발굽을 삼키는데 내 발가락 한없이
쓸쓸한 줄 모르고 꽃들은 자꾸 그렇게 피고 지는 것일까

AND BLINKS

If I ran into you
I wouldn't recognize you, I don't think.
Collecting the groceries and
opening my purse and paying
and rummaging in my pockets wondering what I forgot,
as if leaving that place.

Sometimes,
when a pain that I can't locate
shoots through me, I take aspirin
and bang my face into my pillow—
trying to sleep,
trying to sleep and then

the stain on the ceiling rides the wall and spreads,
and my knees creak and my cough rattles.
Why? Why this?
Really, why does it have to be like this, I say,
pawing the air, and then not.

One day a peony big as a soup bowl
blooms without sound
and blinks a few times like the eyes of an obedient animal
and falls, and lies down—
even if I think there were a day like this,
when it was or what it signified,
I don't know.

껌벅이다가

느닷없이 너 마주친다 해도
그게 무엇인지 알아채지 못할 것 같다
물건을 고르고
지갑 열고 계산을 치루고
잊은 게 없나 주머니 뒤적거리다
그곳을 떠나듯

가끔
손댈 수 없이
욱신거리면 진통제를 먹고
베게에 얼굴을 박고
잠들려고
잠들려고 그러다가

젖은 천정의 얼룩이 벽을 타고 번져와
무릎 삐걱거리고 기침 쿨럭이다가
왜 그럴까 왜 그럴까
도대체 왜 그래야 할까
헛손질만 하다가 말듯이

대접만한 모란이 소리없이 피어나
순한 짐승의 눈처럼 꽃술 몇 번 껌벅이다가
떨어져 누운 날
언젠가도 꼭 이날 같았다는 생각
한다 해도
그게 언제인지 무엇인지 모르겠고

Even if the street corner crumbled
and I bumped into you,
I couldn't pick up everything that fell,
I couldn't possibly recover;
every day was like that and that day too—
I blinked,
rummaged in my pockets;
I left that place.

길 모퉁이 무너지며 너
맞닥뜨린다 해도
쏟아뜨린 것 주워 담을 수 없어
도저히 돌이킬 수 없어
매일이 그렇듯이 그날도
껌벅거리다
주머니 뒤적거리다
그냥 자리를 떠났듯이

A TOWN WITH A TRUMPET CREEPER

I lived as a blind fish. There was a time when I pulled out my fins and hid in the shade of a boulder, having been sick a long while. Yes, so—on bright days like this, my tears welled up clearly, and one side of my heart had a dull pain.

The town is called Wanggung-ni, King's Palace. The deep shade of its stone pagoda causes the trumpet creeper to bloom. A fat chicken totters, searching the shade for feed and, to the sound of the cicada falling like a waterfall, I descend into a deep sleep. The town is made of toppled stones, and there is a small gate.

The echo from each golden trumpet blossom spreads tranquilly, reaching for the end of the sky. A king lived in Wanggung-ni and a queen too, when the rustling of the courtesans' hems covered the deep shadows,

when I would listen to everything from beneath the dark precipice of the boulder. Tears streamed quietly from my blind eyes, and I dreamt that once—later, much later—when this darkness flowed out to where it could almost touch the sky, I would see those bright flowers blooming like the sound of the trumpets.

능소화가 있는 마을

눈 먼 물고기로 살았습니다 지느러미를 떼내고 바위 그늘에 숨어 오래 앓은
적이 있었습니다 그래 이런 부신 날에는 맑은 눈물이 솟고 가슴 한쪽이
뻐근해지는 것입니다

마을 이름은 왕궁리입니다 돌탑의 깊은 그늘이 능소화를 피워 올립니다 살찐
닭이 뒤뚱거리며 그늘을 뒤지고 매미 소리 폭포처럼 쏟아져 또 깊은 잠에
빠져듭니다 무너진 돌무더기의 마을 작은 문

능소화가 하늘 끝까지 뻗쳐 오르고 금빛 꽃송이마다 나팔 소리 잔잔히 울려
퍼졌습니다 왕궁에는 왕이 살았고 왕비가 살았고 시녀들의 긴 옷자락 끄는
소리 깊은 그늘을 덮을 때 그 때

캄캄한 바위 절벽 아래서 나는 다 듣고 있었습니다 먼 눈으로 가만히 눈물
흘려버리고 나중에 나중에 이 어둠 흘러가 하늘에 닿을 때쯤 저 나팔
소리처럼 피어나는 환한 꽃을 보리라 보리라 꿈 꾼 적이 있었습니다

WINDOW WASHER

There, he's comfy.
There, he even smokes a cigarette

and watches time
falling a minute later like the leaves of the white-charcoal tree.

Thick ropes wave all day
as soapy black water descends;
fastened to a rope twenty-four stories up a glass wall, he hoses things down.

He must have ridden a camel
through the eye of a needle
or a herring flying across the sands of a desert into the sky.

He crawled up the steep cliff.
To lift off gently
when a wind rose out of a valley
in the forest of buildings.

And he walked for a long time.
Not even one ant would appear there
but he toed the blade-
edge of that cliff where time stops

and the sun crashed in to the glass wall brightly
and those who looked up, heads crooked:
—Ah, it's so bright!
The instant they rubbed their eyes,
he couldn't be seen.

유리 닦는 남자

그는 거기서 잘 있다
그는 거기서 담배도 한대 피우고

시간이 금세
백탄나무 잎새처럼 지는 걸 본다
종일 유리창엔 굵은 밧줄이 흔들거리고
비누 거품 검은 물 흘러내리고
24층 유리벽 밧줄에 묶여 물줄기를 쏴댄다

약대를 타고 바늘구멍에 들거나
모래사막을 건너 청어를 타고
하늘을 날아야 했다
깎아지른 벼랑을 기어올랐다
빌딩 숲 계곡으로부터
바람이 치켜불기 시작할 때
훌쩍 날아가 보려고

오래도 걸었다
개미 한 마리 얼씬하지 않는
시간이 정지된 벼랑 끝
칼날을 딛고

햇빛이 눈부시게 유리벽을 때리고
고개가 꺾어지게 쳐다보던 사람들이
아 눈부셔
잠시 눈을 비빈 사이
정말 그가 보이지 않았다

THE ABSENT TREE

The name of that tree is dark.
I saw only the sun burning in it
for a moment,
grazing over it like lightning.
White-charcoal tree, heavenly tree, tree of emptiness—
none of these names exist;

the names are not in it…

Arriving
after the sun surfaced slowly,
after the multitudes flowed by,
coming over and over the clouds,

having fallen into underpass of my sleep
to emerge,
after the splash,
above my head,
it stood
for a moment;

that tree—
Once
it was the burning star at my fingertips,
the beast boiling in my throat,
the bird I let fly away when the drought
of my body had finished.

없 는 나 무

그 나무의 이름은 깜깜하다
나무 속에서 타던 해만
잠깐 보았다
번개처럼 스쳐갔다
백탄나무 천상나무 허공나무
없다
그들 속에 그 이름 없다

태양이 죽죽 떠오른 다음
만상이 흘려 간 다음
왔다
구름을 건너 건너 왔다

잠의 지하도를 막 빠져 나와
머리 위에
물보라를 뿜은 다음
잠깐
서 있었다

그 나무
언젠가
손끝에서 타던 별이었으나
목젖에서 끓던 맹수였으나
내 몸의 가뭄 끝에 날려보낸 새였으나

SNOW

I built a house in a snowflake but
it vanished.
It quivered on a branch,
sighing,
and the roof flew away.
I set that bird
cut from a postcard
in a desk drawer
in a corner room
in that house
but it took the house
and flew away.
It's been many years since
the bird with the wings of the size of fingernails
dragged away that house.
It must be exhausted by now.
The snow must keep falling.

눈

눈송이 속에 집을 하나 지었는데
사라졌다
나뭇가지 위에서
한숨쉬며 흔들리다
지붕이 날아간 거다
그 집 구석방에
책상 서랍 속에
카드에서 오려낸
새를 하나 넣어 두었는데
그 집을 데리고 날아간 거다
벌써 십수년을
손톱만한 날개의 새가
그 집을 끌고 날아다니자니
힘들겠다
눈이 자꾸 와야 하는데

HOTEL CALIFORNIA, A PUDDLE

Hotel California
Trapped by it for a while, I hummed the song.
The smell of colitas, shimmering light, as if touching my head,
a woman stood in the doorway,
and, just then, a bell rang out in the distance.

Hey, how did you manage to get here?
Did you think it was the platform at Taejŏn Station?
or *Hotel California*?
You're a tadpole in the stagnant water beside the road after a monsoon,

crazily stirring the surface
which shoots sunlight back like bullets.
"Cabbages! Radishes! Onions!"
When the peddler's wheels splashes through water
in that swoon,

the brilliant puddle,
the moment's *Hotel California*,
thunder falling vaguely from behind the clouds,
some dances remembered, others forgotten,
in the puddle, in the *Hotel,*

someone has left you there and gone
so you listen alone.
Welcome. A prisoner here,
you can check out any time you like but you can never leave.

"Cabbages! Radishes! Onions!"
you won't forget the sound of it,
cast into the midday air,
until the puddle is sent flying to the sun.

웅덩이 호텔 캘리포니아

호텔 캘리포니아
한 동안 그 노래에 갇혀 흥얼거렸지
콜리타꽃 향기, 희미한 불빛, 내 머리를 만져주듯
한 여자 문 앞에 서 있었고
그 순간 멀리서 종소리도 울려왔고

어찌어찌 여기까지 왔는가
대전 역쯤의 플랫폼인 줄 알았는가
호텔 캘리포니아인 줄 알았는가
장마 뒤 길바닥 고인 물에 올챙이

햇빛을 총알처럼 되쏘는 그 속을
미친듯 휘젓고 다니다가
"배추요, 무요, 양파요"
행상의 바퀴가 고인 물 튀기며 지나갈 때
잠시 혼절한 그 때

찬란한 웅덩이, 잠깐의 호텔 캘리포니아
구름 뒤에 천둥소리 아득하게 떨어지고
어떤 춤은 기억되고 어떤 춤은 잊혀지는
웅덩이 호텔 캘리포니아에서

누군가 떨구고 간 너
혼자서 듣고 있지
"어서 오세요. 당신은 이곳의 포로
언제든 떠날 수 있다지만 결코 떠나지 못할 걸요"

한낮의 허공으로 솟구치는
"배추요, 무우요, 양파요오"
그 소리 잊지 못할 걸요
햇빛에 웅덩이 날아가 버리도록

DEER CLIMBING A BAMBOO POLE

Laundry flew on the clothes-line
and the deer ran across with it.
Back then, we could hear them
climbing the bamboo pole to play the *haegŭm*.
We listened, and then listened again.
Evening dove into the earthenware pots,
aging the wine.
The eaves tilted, the fields tilted,
they listened together, didn't they?
Back then, June and peonies,
plum blossoms and blue-birds
were falling in love.
That was the season, wasn't it,
when streams strewn with peach blossoms laid eggs?
The eggs laid words and the words laid eggs.
Back then, the king was born from an egg, wasn't he?
He also heard the deer
climbing the bamboo pole
and playing the *haegŭm*.
He listened and then
climbed up to cry with them, didn't he?
Back then, there was *yalli yalli yallangsŏng.*
There was *yallari yalla…*

사슴이 장대에 올라

빨래줄에 빨래가 날면
사슴도 줄을 타고 함께 뛰었지
그때만 해도
사슴이 장대에 올라 해금을 켜는 걸
들었지
듣다가 듣다가
항아리 속으로 저녁이 뛰어들어
술을 익혔지
처마가 기울고 들판이 기울어
함께 들었지
그 때만 해도
유월은 목단하고
매화는 파랑새하고
연애했지
복사꽃 뜬 냇물이
알을 낳던 시절이었지
알이 말을 낳고 말이 또 알을 낳고
그때만 해도
왕은 알에서 나왔지
왕도
사슴이 장대에 올라 해금을 켜는 걸
들었지
듣다가 장대에 올라 함께 울었지
그때만 해도
얄리 얄리 얄랑성이 있었지
얄라리 얄라가 있었지

SPRING RAIN SHOWER

Hazy, white and big. Without a head or a tail. Running for us in the air from a distance. It overtakes a newly-budding tree, and is quick to pin down the noise of the trolley wheels: Tŏkku! Tŏkku! Tŏkku!…

I was wearing rain gear… It was in front of the last stop, in Sin'gil-dong… In the sudden fog, who could tell front from back?

No, Mother, what are you doing all of a sudden? Wake up! Collect yourself. Collect—… Baby, the phone. Call… How? The ambulance…

A girl who is just starting her first period crumples the letter into her bag and stands there for a long time.

Before her eyes, a silent hazy nothing, no sound, no…

While magnolia blossoms blanket the hospital garden in white, a really big dog-fog swoops down on the street cleaner's cart, on his yellow cap and vest, his boots.

봄 소나기

부옇고 커다란 것이 머리도 꼬리도 없는 것이 멀리서 허공을 달려온 것이 이제
막 새순을 뿜는 나무 한 채를 해치우고
달리던 전차 바퀴 소리를 덕구야 덕구야 덕구야 다급하게 덮치......

우비를 쓰고...... 신길동 전차 종점 앞이었는데..... 느닷없는 안개가 전혀
앞뒤를 분간할 수가

아니 어머니 왜 이러셔요 갑자기 일어나세요 정신차리세요 정신 얘야 전화가
전화를 어떻게 구급차......

이제 초경을 시작한 여자애가 편지를 책가방 속에 구겨 넣고 오랫동안 서서

눈 앞이 부옇게 아무 것도 아무 소리도 아무런......

목련 꽃 송이가 병원 뜰 앞을 다 덮어버리도록 하얗고 커다란 개가 느닷없이
청소부의 수레를 그의 노란 모자를 조끼를 장화를 덥석 덥석

FOREST

Does the path leading to one tree
go like this to another?
Does it finally arrive
at all the ultimate trees?

The ideal beauty of one tree
is so much like that of another.

No end and no beginning.

Green quivering
for a moment—
whose shadow are you?

숲

한 나무에게 가는 길은
다른 나무에게도 이르게 하니?
마침내
모든 아름다운 나무에 닿게도 하니?

한 나무의 아름다움은
다른 나무의 아름다움과 너무 비슷해

처음도 없고 끝도 없고

푸른 흔들림
너는 잠시
누구의 그림자니?

MIRROR, MIRROR AND
MIRROR IN THE MIRROR

Over my forehead I saw a hill.
Was there a small field—something like a window—
on that hill?
Was it real?
Did naked trees stand in a row near the station?
Did I stand carrying a baby
on my back then too,
where cold, empty-handed men returned
with just the bones
of the big fish they had stripped of its flesh?
As if I were trapped
in the mirror in the mirror in the mirror in the mirror,
was I in some other life,
absorbed at some other time
far away,
in scenery like this?
I piled up the useless past in my body.
In front of me,
cars flow on and on…
It's been so long since the baby on my back cried himself to sleep—
So long. So long ago
I'm not sure
if a wind blew then too?
Was the ancient paper shredded in my body
and I heard its rustling sound
as wind
slapped one side of my face?
Birds
unable to open their eyes in the cold
fly toward dark places,
trying to rise in the distance,
crying out.

거울 속에 거울 거울 거울

이마 위로는 산이 보이고
산 위에는 창문처럼
작은 밭이 있었던가
그랬던가
정거장 끝으로 헐벗은 나무들 늘어섰던가
그때도
애를 업고 섰었던가
빈 손의 추운 남자들 大魚의 살 다
뜯긴 채
뼈만 끌고 돌아오는 곳
거울 속에 거울 속에 거울 속에 거울
속에 갇힌 것처럼
다른 생의
언젠가 아득한 곳에서도
이런 똑같은 풍경 속에 잠겨 있었던가
쓸데없이
지나간 시간들을 내 몸에 쌓아두고
차들이 내 앞으로 흘러 흘러
가고
업힌 아이 울다 잠든지 오래고
오래고 오래 전이라서
뚜렷하진 않지만
그 때도 바람이 불었던가
바람이
내 얼굴 한쪽을 때리면
내 몸에서 삭은 종이 부서져
가라앉는 소리 났던가
새들
추워 눈 못 뜨고
깜깜한 곳으로 아득하게
날아 날아 오르려고
울면서

WINDOW

Those are poplars over there.
No, the two ears of a donkey.
They are two leafless poplars.
No, the two ears of an old donkey.

Blood-colored twilight had faded.
A man leans in the window muttering.

By the window, an old donkey has come to stand.

So far to go!
How will he push
through the fog
pulling those feeble wheels
with bags piled as high as mountains?

He heads for the glass.
He'd been trapped for so long—
He punches through the hard darkness; he runs and runs.

The poplars in the dark
shudder and fly off.

Oh, they can't fly.
That donkey caught in the square of the window
with his two stupid ears,

they aren't poplars over there.
Two warped wheels cast aside.
A body screaming
that's, that's a black sword slashing down.

창

저건 포플라 나무다
아니 저건 나귀의 두 귀다
저건 잎진 포플라 두 그루다
아니 분명 늙은 나귀의 두 귀다

핏빛 노을은 다 지나갔다
그는 유리창에 매달려 중얼댄다

유리창엔 늙은 나귀가 와 섰다

아득히 멀다
안개 속을
짐을
산처럼 잔뜩 싣고
저 허약한 바퀴로
어떻게 헤쳐가나

유리창 속으로
그는 달아나려 한다
너무 오래 갇혀 있었다
딱딱한 어둠을 뚫고 뛴다 뛴다

어둠 속에 포플라 나무
진저리를 치고 날아오른다

오, 날아 오르지 못한다
사각의 유리창에 갇힌
나귀, 이리석은 두 귀

저건 포플라 나무가 아니다
팽개쳐 일그러진 두 바퀴
소리치는 몸뚱이
저건 저건 내리치는 검은 칼

A THICKET OF WILD ROSES

You were among the thorns of the wild roses, weren't you? You saw me, huh? as if looking this way from in front of the thicket. Between me and the roses, a narrow path curved up a hill. Behind me, a stream tumbled in the valley. I pretended to look sideways at the flowers. I couldn't look straight at you. No, I never saw you. You didn't know, or you pretended you didn't. Should I tell you that I was stabbed by your thorns for a long time? What should I do? And then it all just washed past, you know? And then I left you there with thorns in your eyes, in your ears, in your forehead—your whole body a thicket of thorns.

One day I woke to find that I had been washed too far away. Horse-dung-cow-dung beetles—rolling and tumbling and fumbling, face-first in the shit—push across the open fields. Cars flow by noisily on roads with their lights on. I breathe hard, blinking my black eyes. I will close them soon. Heading somewhere in a speeding ambulance, even before I reach the big river, there is not even the slightest memory of the thicket. Tiny petals drift in intervals, but the prickling pain, I don't know—I just can't know—what it is.

찔레가시덤불

    당신은 찔레가시 속에 있었지요 찔레덤불 앞에서 이쪽으로 눈길을 주고 있는 것처럼 보였지요 찔레덤불과 나 사이엔 조붓한 길이 굽어 산을 오르고 등뒤로는 산골짝 물이 요란하게 뒤집히며 흘러가고 나는 당신을 똑바로 못보고 비스듬히 찔레덤불만 보는 척 하고 아니 나는 당신을 한번도 본 적이 없고 당신은 아무 것도 모르고 모른 척 하고 내가 당신의 가시에 오래 찔리고 있었다는 걸 전해야 하나 어쩌나 그러다가 다 흘러갔지요 그러다가 당신의 눈 당신의 귀 당신의 이마 온통 찔레가시덤불인 채로 두고

어느 날 보니 나는 멀리도 흘러 왔겠지요 말똥구리 소똥구리 말똥을 굴리며 엎어지며 고꾸라지며 들판을 건너가고 불켠 차들이 요란하게 흘러가는 거리를 지나가고 있겠지요 가쁜 숨을 내쉬다 검은 눈을 껌뻑거리다 이내 눈을 감겠지요 달리는 구급차 속에서 어딘가로 가기는 가는데 큰 강에 이르기도 전에 세상에 찔레덤불 기억조차 없고 이따금 자잘한 꽃잎 떠내려 오지만 아무 것도 모르겠고 따끔따끔한 이것 무슨 일인지 알 수가 없고

ANGEL

Once, I desperately wanted to buy a gun.
I don't know how I could forget that.
I wanted to go to Pusan to buy it.
I wanted to borrow some money, to buy a boat and head into the desert.

An angel at one point,
and a thicket of wild roses, and dynamite—
I don't know how he disappeared.

Now he's not in my mind
he's not in the rock or in the storm
or in the puddle either.

He doesn't know he disappeared.
The idiot. He doesn't know he was an angel once.
He vanished so deeply
that I dug and dug into the abandoned mine inside myself—
but still he's not there.

All by myself, I hold a lighter in front of the puddle and,
shivering, shine the light into it, but it's murky again,

the puddle where I'll see his reflection.
If I—the only miner who can dig him up—
disappear,
he will have been nothing from the beginning.
If I—the only witness
who knew him to be a radiant angel—
disappear,
this world would vanish.

천 사

간절히 총을 사고 싶은 적이 있었다
어찌어찌 그 생각을 잊었는지 모른다
총을 사러 부산엘 가겠다고
돈을 꾸고 배를 사서 사막으로 뜨겠다고

한때 천사였던
한때 덤불찔레였고 한때 폭약이었던
그가 어떻게 사라져 버렸는지 모른다

지금 내 마음 속에 없고
돌 속에도 폭풍 속에도
물웅덩이 속에도 없다

그는 그가 사라진 줄을 모른다
한때 천사였던 것도 모른다
너무나 깊숙이 사라졌기에
버려진 폐광의 내 속을 캐고 캐도
그는 이제 없다

나 혼자 라이타를 들이대는 웅덩이
떨면서 비추고 다시 일그러뜨린다

그를 비춰볼 웅덩이
그를 파낼 유일한 광부인
나조차 사라지면
그는 아예 없었던 게 된다
그가 잠시 찬란한 천사였던 걸
증거할 자도
세상 천지도

ON THE WAY TO BUY MEAT

It looked like I was going to buy some meat and was on my way.
Someone said I had to get it from that store.
I went past the fake fish pond behind the church
to arrive at the place
near where *Susŏng kalbi* was written,
but that wasn't it.
I had to go farther.
Where a heap of yellow earth crumbled,
children were catching ants.
Where the ant laid her white eggs,
they were looking for the queen.
One kid touched an ant's behind to his tongue
and was shuddering.
I was just thinking: *I need to get the meat and go home.*
Everything was quiet.
Trees leaned over,
as if a big storm were passing though.
Windows were closed soundlessly.
Blood-colored water
flowed in the gutters.
I was on my way to buy meat.
The kids were face down.
They slept,
speechless, blood smeared on their lips.
They were the ones I had seen in the newspaper.
Those who kept the chaff of the rice and wild fruits in their pockets—
someone said they were spies.
I was lost on my way to buy meat
and been captured there too.
I needed to be awakened.
The rain outside—
it was blood-colored.

고기 사러 갔던 길

고기를 사러 간다고 가는 길이었다
꼭 그집 고기를 사오라 했다
교회 뒤 인공낚시터를 지나
수성갈비라고 쓴 옆
그 집은 가보니 아니었다
한참을 더 가야했다
황토 흙이 무너져 내리는 곳에서
아이들이 개미를 잡고 있었다
개미가 하얗게 알을 낳아 놓은 곳에서
여왕개미를 찾고 있었다
한 아이가 개미 꽁무니에 혀를 대보고
진저리를 치고 있었다
고기를 사서 빨리 집에 가야 하는데
생각뿐이었다
사방이 지나치게 고요했다
거대한 폭풍이 지나간 듯
나무들이 길게 쓰러져 있었다
창문들이 소리없이 닫히고
개천을 흐르는 물이 핏빛이었다
고기를 사러 가는 중이었다
아이들이 엎드려 있었다
입가에 피를 묻히고 아무 말도 못하고
잠들어 있었다
신문에서 본 그들이었다
주머니에서 산열매와 벼이삭이 나왔던
간첩이라고 했다
고기를 사러 간다고 가서는
길을 잃은 나도 거기 붙들려 있었다
깨워야했다
밖은 비가 오고 있었다
핏빛이었다

CANNA AND THE SWORD

You held the hilt,
and yes, I was quick to stick out my neck.
You're the one holding it, not me;
I'm the one watching the blade swing,
not you.

At the very end of our conversation
the canna's just starting to fall.

It falls for the canna
to win the canna.

Close and lock the door;
let's be sad to our heart's content.
Sadness the first day,
and the second too.
The third day, still sadness.
Let's watch the sadness of the first day tumble into the sadness of the
    second day
and the sadness of the second day tumble into the sadness of the third day
and sadness of the third day collapse again
into the sadness of the fourth.

The noodles at the wake swell;
the deer in flower cards jump.
Those who are crying fall silent
and slurp their noodles.

Let's collapse to the end
for sadness
that can't last.
Let's watch it
tumble for the canna.

칼과 칸나꽃

너는 칼자루를 쥐었고
그래 나는 재빨리 목을 들이민다
칼자루를 쥔 것은 내가 아닌 너이므로
휘두르는 칼날을 바라봐야 하는 것은
네가 아닌 나이므로

너와 나 이야기의 끝장에 마침
막 지고 있는 칸나꽃이 있다

칸나꽃이 칸나꽃임을 이기기 위해
칸나꽃으로 지고 있다

문을 걸어 잠그고
슬퍼하자 실컷
첫날은 슬프고
둘째 날도 슬프고
셋째 날 또한 슬플 테지만
슬픔의 첫째 날이 슬픔의 둘째 날에게 가 무너지고
슬픔의 둘째 날이 슬픔의 셋째 날에게 가 무너지고
슬픔의 셋째 날이 다시 쓰러지는 걸
슬픔의 넷째 날이 되어 바라보자

상가집의 국수발은 불어터지고
화투장의 사슴은 뛴다
울던 사람은 통곡을 멈추고
국수발을 빤다

오래 가지 못하는 슬픔을 위하여
끝까지 쓰러지자
슬픔이 칸나꽃에게로 가
무너지는 걸 바라보자

ROOM

In front of that room, there is a big tree blocking the window. When dawn comes, a thousand birds arrive to chirp in that tree. The tree weeps like the swirling of a stream. Each leaf becomes a bird and shakes itself. To appease the one window, the tree drops all its leaves.

There is a man sleeping like the dead in that room. There is a man who piles up time in his body. He doesn't know that the tree came to stand in front of the window. He can't hear it weep. There is a man in the world,— who tries to extinguish the fire in his chest but has turned utterly to ash. In that room, he is there, lying down.

방

    그 방 앞에는 창을 가리는 커다란 나무가 있다 새벽이면 그 나무에 천마리의 새가 날아와 지저귄다 시냇물의 소용돌이처럼 나무가 운다 나뭇잎 하나하나 새가 되어 뒤흔든다 창문 하나를 달래 보겠다고 나무는 제 잎을 다 떨군다

그 방 안에는 죽음 같은 잠을 자는 이가 있다 제 몸에 시간을 쌓아두는 이가 있다 그이는 창 앞에 나무가 와 섰는 줄을 모른다 그이는 나무가 우는 소리를 못 듣는다 세상에는 가슴 속 불꽃을 재우려다 아주 재가 되어 버린 이가 있다 그 방에 그이가 누워 있다

A FOREST OF DONKEY EARS

More and more time drifted by;
I had lost you long before,
and what I hesitated to say, buried in my mind,
became the language of fish,
the language of little dogs.

The redpoll between the new leaves,
those purple flowers in the vines of arrowroot,
those things, those words
break open, split open, and bloom.
But just as I can't hear
what they mean,

they want to belong in every country,
want to be born again.

If I show up years later and the words
burst abruptly from my mouth,
will you hear them—
is it too sudden for you?

Like understanding the cry of the redpoll
only as the red of berries,

like something heard before
with a knitted brow—
Who was it? What was it?

당나귀 귀의 숲

시간은 무장무장 흘러버렸고
당신을 잃은지 오래 되었고
망설이다 묻어둔 그 말
물고기의 말이 되었고
강아지의 말이 되었고

잎사귀 틈에 홍방울새
칡 덩굴 속에 자주 꽃
그것들 그말들
비집고 비집고 돋아난 것인데
도대체 무슨 뜻인지
내가 알아듣지 못하는 것처럼

그 말 모든 나라에 속하고 싶고
다시 태어나고만 싶어

그래 수년 만에 나타나 불쑥
입밖에 낸다면
당신 그 소리 느닷없어 알아 들을까

홍방울새 울음소리
빨갛게 맺는
열매로만 알아듣는 것처럼

언젠가 들은 소리라고
이마를 찌프리고
누구였더라 무엇이었더라

will you understand the tangled things
these tangled things, and know what they mean?

I crawl toward the mountaintop,
rushing to the sandstorm,
pouring words into the cracks of boulders—

they become a chattering thicket of bamboo
in an instant, calling the empty wind.

Where do I take the sound to comfort it?
What should I call it?

엉기고 엉겨버린 것들
알아 볼 수 있을까

산꼭대기로 기어 올라가서
모래폭풍 속으로 달려나가서
바위구멍 속에 퍼부어 두었던 말들

대숲이 되어 수런거리는데
순간에 빈 바람을 부르는데

어디로 데려가 달래주나
어디로 어떻게 불어보나

WITH A MOUNTAINSIDE CHERRY TREE
AND THE SHADOW OF A WOMAN

He took a mountainside cherry tree and the shadow of a woman
to live with him.
He didn't have any money, any wife or children or house.
He was old, of course.
He crawled out from something like an oyster shell among the boulders
and sat for a long while.
He paced.
He realized spring had come
after seeing the cherry tree hang down so listlessly.
He washed a pot
and then held the shadow of a woman who lay ill;
he set her out in the sun,
spreading the light and laying it over her.
And she, thin as sheet of paper, grew old and white too.
A few blossoms hanging down like the sandman in a blind girl's eyes
from the mountainside cherry tree.
Her forehead and cheeks were warm.
No, chilly actually.
This spring cannot be trusted.
Heat waves bloom where she was laid down,
she flies slowly away.
The cherry tree is so old, hardly two petals dangle and fly away.
Spring leaves once more.
She was not a woman of this world;
But he couldn't help living that way,
with the mountainside cherry tree and the shadow of a woman.

산벚꽃나무하고 여자 그림자하고

그는 산벚꽃나무와 여자 그림자 하나
데리고 살지요
그는 돈도 없고 처자도 없고 집도 없고
그는 늙었지요
바위 구멍 굴딱지같은 곳에서 기어나와
한참을 앉아 있지요
서성거리지요
산벚꽃나무 기운없이 늘어진 걸 보니
봄이 왔지요
냄비를 부시다 말고
앓아 누운 여자 그림자를 안아다
양지쪽에 눕히고
햇빛을 깔고 햇빛을 덮어주고
종잇장같이 얇은 그녀도 하얗게 늙어가지요
산벚꽃나무 장님처녀 눈곱 달 듯
한두 송이 꽃 매달지요
그녀의 이마가 그녀의 볼이 따뜻하지요
아니 차디차지요
이 봄은 믿을 수가 없지요
그녀를 눕혔던 자리 아지랑이 피어 오르고
그녀가 천천히 날아가지요
산벚꽃나무 너무 늙어 겨우 꽃잎
두장 매달았다 떨구지요
또 봄은 가지요
그녀는 세상에 없는 여자고
그래도 그는 그렇게밖에 살 수 없지요
산벚꽃나무하고 여자 그림자하고

A DANCE WITH THE WALL

The red leaves of the daimyo oak have a crush on the wall.
The tree's shadows sway over it.

They don't know what
they are looking for
or what they touch.

The surface of the wall is pale and
hard in the glow of the evening;

the oak coughs
on the surface of the wall as it tries to escape,
pushing its whole being, its heartbreak and hipbone.

Embracing a boundless hunger,
and the game it plays with the oak,

the surface of the wall doesn't know what dances inside it.
It doesn't know what's growing hot.

The oak comes looking
and falls forward, slipping.

Dazed
dusk rushes over.

벽과의 춤을

떡갈나무 붉은 이파리의 짝사랑은 담벼락이다
떡갈나무 그림자 벽에 너울거린다

자신이 찾는 것이
자신이 만지는 것이 무엇인지
모른다

노을 속에 담벼락은
창백하고 딱딱하고

자꾸 달아나려는 담벼락에
떡갈나무 기침을 쏟아놓는다
가슴병을 허리뼈를 밀어넣는다

헤아릴 수 없는 배고픔을 안고
그와 하는 놀이

담벼락은 자기 속에 감춘 것을 모른다
뜨거워진 것도 모른다

떡갈나무는 찾느라고
미끄러지고 엎어지는데

정신없이
땅거미가 밀려온다

HER LIPS ARE WARM WHILE YOURS ARE COLD

So
Please release me, let me go, I don't love you anymore, please....

When I load low fat milk, mackerel, Kleenex, rubber gloves
into my trunk and slam it shut....
Please release me drifts my way in an endlessly smooth voice.
A dog howls and claws at the window of a car parked across the street.

"In this country, the dahlias are as big as serving trays, the cherry
    blossoms are fist-sized,
and they don't wilt,
they bloom one month, then two, and...."
when Ŭn-yŏng is on the phone

when the car beside me suddenly comes close and hits mine.
The driver leaps out:
"Lady, I was turning here.
What were you thinking, swerving like that?"
The song doesn't know how to stop.

A man returns a shopping cart—to get the coin deposit—doesn't return.
Ŭn-yŏng doesn't hang up the phone.

"No. You suddenly cranked your wheel while I was turning!"
He ignores me, takes out white spray paint and paints
lines on the road.

그녀의 입술은 따스하고 당신의 것은 차거든

그러니
제발 날 놓아줘, 당신을 더 이상 사랑하지 않거든, 그러니 제발,

저지방 우유, 고등어, 클리넥스, 도라지나물, 고무장갑을 싣고
트렁크를 꽝 내리닫는데……
부드럽기 그지없는 목소리로 플리즈 릴리즈 미
가 흘러나오네
건너편에 세워둔 차 안에서 개 한 마리 차창을 긁으며 울부짖네

이 나라는 다알리아가 쟁반만 해, 벚꽃도 주먹만 해
지지도 않고
한 달이고 두 달이고 피어만 있다고
은영이가 전화했을 때

느닷없이 옆 차가 다가와 내 차를 꽝 박네
운전수가 튀어나와
아줌마, 내가 이렇게 돌고 있는데
거기서 튀어나오면 어떻게 해
그래도 노래는 멈출 줄을 모르네

쇼핑카트를 반환하러 간 사람, 동전을 뺀다고 가서는 오지를 않네
은영이는 전화를 끊지를 않네

내가 도는데 아저씨가 갑자기 핸들을 꺾었잖아요
듣지도 않고 남자는 재빨리 흰 스프레이를 꺼내
바닥에 죽죽죽 금을 긋네

Ten minutes pass—then twenty; cars still stream out of the
    shopping center.
That song again from the speakers.
To waste life this way would be a sin.
Release me, please, please release me and let me love again

The rice, those greens—same old, same old;
the dahlia as big as a serving tray, the fist-sized cherry blossoms,
the song, that tune—
I bought what I had bought before and packed it away.

"Someone hit me!" I scream;
Ŭn-yŏng doesn't hang up the phone,
sobbing:
"The blueberries are free here; you can go to the patch
and pick a bucketful.
Let's go to Blueberry Hill, bake a blueberry cake."

Please release me, I don't love you any more.
Her lips are warm while yours are cold.
So please, release me and let me love again.

십분이 지나고 이십분이 지나도 쇼핑 센터를 빠져나가는 차들
스피커에선 또 그 노래
이런 삶은 낭비야, 이건 죄악이야,
날 놓아줘, 부탁해, 제발 다시 사랑할 수 있게 날 놓아줘

그 나물에 그 밥
쟁반만한 다알리아에 주먹만한 벚꽃, 그 노래에 그 타령
지난 번에도 산 것을 또 사서 실었네

옆 차가 내 차를 박았단 말이야 소리쳐도
은영이는 전화를 끊지를 않네

훌쩍이면서
여기는 불루베리가 공짜야 공원에 가면
바께쓰로 하나 가득 따 담을 수 있어
불루베리 힐에 놀러가서 불루베리 케잌을 만들자구

플리즈 릴리즈 미, 널 더 이상 사랑하지 않거든
그녀의 입술은 따스하고 당신의 것은 차거든
그러니 제발, 날 놔 줘, 다시 사랑할 수 있게 놓아 달란 말이야

ARABESQUE

He said he tried to rip down my name.
He said he'd do it too.

At the construction site
I saw him take down a concrete floor with a sledge hammer.
He punched a hole with a drill, then sliced through the rebar with a
    cutting-torch.
He roared, suddenly, then cursed and cursed.

Even so
he saw the small bird flying
and told me it was a goldfinch, not a sparrow.

I learned that it was a goldfinch for the very first time.

아 라 베 스 크

그는 내 이름을 끊으려 했다고
끊겠다고 했어요

그가 공사장에서
콘크리트 바닥을 해머로 내리치는 걸 봤어요
드릴로 구멍을 파고 불칼로 쇠를 잘랐어요
그는 느닷없이 소리를 지르고 쌍욕을 해댔어요

그러다가도
날아가던 작은 새를 보고
그것은 참새가 아니라 방울새라고 했어요

나는 그게 방울새인 줄 처음 알았어요

THE *WHALE* SASHIMI RESTAURANT

Who caught the baby whale?
Beneath the restaurants standing in a row,
it is raining,
waves call out before our eyes,
and the whale, not knowing it is dead,
calls out for its mother's breast.
It tries to seize the hem of a skirt.
Slipping away, it floats around,
opening its dead eyes
in the rain.
It catches the hem of a wave
sweeping out to sea.
Its dead mouth opens wide
trying to follow the wave.
Its dead tail and dead fin paddle along.
Rain washes down
the window of the restaurant in streaks.
The edge of the sign,
each branch of the Tree of Heaven,
the whale's forehead, its heart, its guts and flippers,
try to wash away
with the desperation of things that can't.

고래 횟집

누가 고래 새끼를 묶어놓았나
즐비한 횟집 아래
비가 오고
바로 눈앞에서 파도가 부르고
고래는 자기가 죽은 줄도 모르고
엄마 젖을 부르네
빠져나가는 치맛자락 붙잡네
놓치고 헤매다니네
빗속에서
고래는 죽은 눈을 뜨네
떠내려가는 파도자락 붙잡네
죽은 입을 벌리고
흐르려구
죽은 꼬리를 죽은 지느러미를 젓네
빗줄기가
횟집 유리창을 쓸어내리네
간판 가장자리를
가죽나무 가지가지를
이마를 가슴을 창자를 다리를
흐르려구
흐를 수 없는 것들의 간곡함으로
흐르기로 하려구

THE EVENING'S SUPERMARKET

Hey, how are things these days?
—Me? You're asking me?
Can't you see I'm choosing eggs?
My cousin bought some land and struck it rich.
Every night my house is swept away.
Why are eggs so quiet?
The fish were beheaded without a second thought;
My mother often got lost in the street.
I wish she would stay home and wear her hearing aid.
If she'd just answer the phone.
My cousin bought some land
and my stomach aches with envy;
there is no way to convey this.
I want someone to stand there, but who?
Is spinach always this limp?
There are too many things to buy.
Hey, how are things these days?
I want to buy Gatsby himself.
Wasn't he ruined while holding a bouquet of roses?
I'd like to buy something—even the eyes of an owl
do you know where those are sold?
Mr. Korea, on every single t-shirt:
are you asking me?

저녁의 수퍼마켓

이봐요, 사는 게 어때요?
나, 나 말인가요?
달걀을 고르고 있잖아요.
사촌은 땅을 사서 벼락부자가 되고
우리 집은 저녁마다 떠내려 가지요.
왜 이렇게 달걀들은 조용한지요
생선은 무심하게 목이 잘리고
엄마는 자주 길을 잃는다는데
보청기나 끼고 계셨으면 좋겠어요
전화하면 제발 받기라도 했으면
사촌은 땅을 샀는데
나는 배가 아프고
전할 길이 없네요
이 자리엔 누구를 세워 둬야 하는지
시금치는 늘 이렇게 시무룩한가요
살 것들은 그득한데
이봐요 사는 게 어떠냐구요?
위대한 개츠비를 사고 싶은데
그는 장미다발을 안고 파멸했지요
부엉이 눈이라도 사고 싶은데
어디서 파나요?
티셔츠 위에 대한민국 씨
지금 내, 내게 묻는 건가요?

RED TUBS

My grandmother's house is not in bellflower fields.
It's a third floor apartment
above *Renaissance Market* and *With a View Realty.*
Beneath the Big Dipper, between the persimmon and the hydrangea,
there is no well.
There's a *Black Rose Video* there.
My uncle's debt hangs over him;
the field at Changt'ŏk is being seized.
The crooked road there is being straightened.
It's the year 2000 at my grandmother's house.
There's a *kimch'i* refrigerator and a water filter in the kitchen.
No mash from the home brew, sticky rice cakes, or *yŏt.*
The scary ditch I jumped over hiding my eyes has vanished,
A motel stands there now
with an Arabian-style roof put on
like a hat on a head.
The mill has become a plastics factory
and its sign reads:
PLASTIC BUCKETS OF ALL KINDS,
WATER TANKS, PAILS, RED TUBS, DOGHOUSES.

빨간 다라이

외가집은 도라지 꽃밭 위에 없다
외가집은 지금
부흥수퍼 전망부동산 위 3층에 있다
북두칠성 아래 감나무와 수국나무 사이
우물도 없다
그 자리엔 흑장미비디오가 있다
외삼촌은 빚더미 위에 있고
장턱거리 밭은 가압류 중이고
구불거렸던 길은 곧게 펴졌다
외가집은 지금 서기 2000년이고
부엌엔 김치냉장고와 정수기가 있고
엿 밥풀강정 술찌게미 따위는 없다
잔치집에서 술 취해 돌아오다
얼어 죽었다는 애꾸 김석출
때문에 무서워 외면하고 건너 뛰던
도랑은 사라졌다
아라비아식 지붕을 모자처럼 올려놓은
모텔이 서 있다
방앗간은 연성공업사가 되었고
간판엔 이렇게 써 있다
각종 플라스틱 통
저수조 물탱크 함지박 빨간다라이 개집

WATERMELON PATCH AND THE MOON

Moonlight, from so far away,
on the watermelon patch,
and in the dark patterns of its furrows,
shining into the motel and the sky-black car
slipping up to it,
and the red car pulling up soundlessly.
The watermelon patch was hot all day long, and now
moonlight
lays the shadows of the poplars down so they
sway in the water of the rice paddies,
growing faint.
Moonlight moves through a place like the flickering consciousness
of dreams, too.
All alone, the watermelons grow rounder and rounder and rounder.
With their leaves,
they row toward the round moon;
in the green and the dappled stripes,
to fill the red rooms inside,
they mumble, *You have no idea*
how long it has taken—
from the black spots of the far off sun to these black seeds—
to find you.
Summer days, winter days, all mixed together,
Yes, moonlight,
thirsty,
on crimson patches in a green ravine.

달과 수박밭

달빛은 참 멀리서도 왔네
수박밭으로
검은 줄무늬 수박고랑으로
달빛은 참
모텔 안으로 까만 차가
미끄러져 들어서고
빨간 차가 또 소리없이 스며드는
거길 비추기도 하지
하루 온종일
수박밭은 뜨거웠는데
달빛은 참
미루나무를 눕히고
골짜기 논물에 미루나무가
누워서 흔들리다 흐려지다
꿈에 들어 혼몽 중인
거길 지나기도 하지
수박은 혼자서
둥글어지고 둥글어지고 둥글어지다
잎사귀로 노를 저어
둥근 달에게
기어 오르기도 하지
달빛은 참
초록으로 얼룩덜룩한 줄무늬 속으로
붉은 방으로 가득 들어차려고
먼 태양 흑점에서부터 수박씨까지
얼마나 오랫동안
너를 만나러 왔는지 몰라 중얼거리며
여름날과 겨울날이 섞여버리도록
목이 말라서
푸른 골짜기 붉은 밭으로
달빛은 참

AN APPLE SELLER SCATTERED IN FRONT OF A *MUSSO*

Say what it was
shining in your eyes,
in those small apples,
in the flutter and sway,
in the trace of crimson and green,
in the sunlight and clouds passing.
Say what vanished
in new red hope bought
with crumpled bills,
in the swagger and wiggle of a hip,
in the child coming to him, crying,
sunset burning in the windows.
Say what scattered, oh,
in the moan of the moment
when the fresh scent of the newly-ripe
apples rose, something also rose with them
on the cart.
Say it—
The birds on the street pull you into a deep sleep
circling in empty air;
the *Musso* stops to stand staring
into your depths,
deep and dark;
over the tops of black apples
opened and still,
what scrapes quietly past,
what hustles to fade away.

무쏘 앞에 흩어진 사과장수

당신 눈 속에
거기 작은 사과 속에
비쳤던 것
붉고 푸른 얼룩
구름과 햇빛이 지나간 흔적
거기 펄럭이던 것
흔들리며 지나간 것
무엇이 있었나 말해봐
노을에 불타는 유리창
구겨져 짠내나는 지폐
새로 산 빨간 희망
엉덩이를 흔들며 뒤뚱거린 것
울면서 다가서는 어린 것
무엇이 또 사라졌나 말해봐
수레 위에 갓 익은 사과알
그 신향기 막 떠오를 때
함께 피어오르던 것
어어 하는 순간에 흩어진 것
말해봐
거리의 새들이 당신의 깊은 잠을 끌고
허공을 한바퀴 도는 중인데
무쏘가 멈춰서서 당신의 깊은
캄캄한 바닥을 들여다 보고 있는데
열린채 멈춰버린 검은 사과 위로
조용히 스쳐 지나간 것
급히도 사라져 버린 것

OLD WOMAN

She was old because she was a baby once.
She was a lark once, and a blade of grass,
so her teeth fell out.
She fell in love once and,
because she laughed like a pear blossom,
she became a fumbling
old woman.
Because she is like a collapsing cane
and her hands shook so,
she was a girl once.
Like the moss rose and the lark,
she had whispered.
A lop-sided gourd.
Strands of white hair—
that's why she can't forget
the red hood left up there,
the wolf,
the stones stuffed in its belly.
She's so thirsty.
She sinks endlessly to the bottom of the well.
She can't stand up.
Because she was a pear blossom, the lark and the grass,
she is an ancient woman now.
An old sack,
ugly
and therefore beautiful.

늙은 여자

한때 아기였기 때문에 그녀는 늙었다
한때 종달새였고 풀잎이었기에
그녀는 이가 빠졌다
한때 연애를 하고
배꽃처럼 웃었기 때문에
더듬거리는
늙은 여자가 되었다
무너지는 지팡이가 되어
손을 덜덜 떨기 때문에
그녀는 한때 소녀였다
채송화처럼 종달새처럼
속삭였다
쭈그렁 바가지
몇가닥 남은 허연 머리카락은
그래서 잊지 못한다
거기 놓였던 빨강 모자를
늑대를
뱃속에 쑤셔 넣은 돌멩이들을
그녀는 지독하게 목이 마르다
우물 바닥에 한없이 가라앉는다
일어설 수가 없다
한때 배꽃이었고 종달새였다가 풀잎이었기에
그녀는 이제 늙은 여자다
징그러운
추악하기에 아름다운
늙은 주머니다

WHILE SLIPPING ON STOCKINGS

As if they have the right,
wives, in a surprise attack,
drag mistresses away by the hair.

So the cliché goes.

It's the same with those who take the souls of the dead.
Just coming home from work,
with three stairs left to climb in front of his house,
a man's heart stops suddenly and he's dragged off.
My brother died that way.

I got the call, broke down, and could only think,
"Let's put time aside
for as long as it takes me to slip on
my stockings,"
as I pulled a pair of stockings
over my stockings
and I was taken away.

스타킹을 신는 동안

당연히 그럴 권리가 있다는 듯이
본처들은 급습해
첩의 머리끄뎅이를 끌고 간다

상투적 수법이다

저승사자도 마찬가지다
퇴근해 돌아오는 사람을
집 앞 계단을 세 칸 남겨놓고
갑자기 심장을 멈추게 해 끌고 가버린다
오빠가 그렇게 죽었다

전화를 받고 허둥대다가
스타킹을 신는
그 동안만이라도 시간을 유예하자고
고작 그걸 아이디어라고
스타킹 위에 또 스타킹을 신고
끌려가고 있었다

BLOOD

Half of my blood is grandmother's.
Bent over at the waist like a *kiyŏk*, her bones
became the bent bones of my back.
Those that hugged me, those that cast me away,
those that struck my cheek, they live together
in me.
Those that make soup in me,
those that pound nails, those that blossom light,
Grandmother,
the moss rose blooming in thick bunches beneath the window;
everything pretty in my eyes
is because of the polished candlestick and the flame that bloomed
in your blood.
They say that the day you died,
Grandfather just swept the yard.
When I suffer from a closed sense of contempt
become a bug and cry,
sprout as a poisonous mushroom,
want to become thin as a snake,
it's because of your blood.
The roar of the world behind the haze of dust,
that ringing in my ear,
Grandmother (deaf in one ear
because you were struck there once and your eardrum burst),
that ringing in mine is on account of the blood that swirled ringing
in yours.

피

내 피의 반은 할머니 피다
허리가 기역자로 꺾였던
할머니 뼈는 내 굽은 등뼈가 되었다
나를 안아준 나를 팽개친
내뺨을 갈긴 이들이 내 속엔
함께 산다
내 속에서 국을 끓이는 이
못을 박는 이 불을 피우는 이
할머니다
창 아래 오종종 피어난 채송화
내 눈에 이쁜 것도
촛대를 닦아 꽃불을 피우던
할머니 피 때문이다
할머니 죽던 날
할아버지 마당만 쓱쓱 쓸었다 한다
억울하게 능멸당하면
벌레가 되어 울다가
독버섯으로 피었다가
뱀처럼 가늘어지고 싶은 거
할머니 피 때문이다
매맞아 고막이 터져 한쪽 귀가 멀었던 할머니
세상의 굉음들이 아득한 먼지 뒤에서
내 귀에 쟁쟁거리는 거
할머니 귀 속에서
소용돌이 치며 울던 피 때문이다

LEBANESE EMOTION

Even when they're piled at the store, watermelons ripen.
And when they can't ripen anymore, they grow old.
Trapped with its black lines,
burnt, its insides
crimson, the seeds of my heart are black.
They don't speak. Of course, they can't.
Shall I call it
Lebanese emotion?

Donkeys loaded with watermelons leave.
Bells clinking among the boulevards of trembling poplars
at the Taklamakan desert oasis—
they still use donkeys there.
In the big markets, craftsmen of silver and gold
bend over their rings; they want to become something.

Wanting to become what cannot be,
they die there, and I die here.
They lived there and I lived here.

Lived. Did I? In the desert?
In Lebanon?

Veiled women pass by
against a background of buildings pocked by bombs exploding.
Hollowed eyes flashing; they come and go like gulls;
Maybe it was me.

레바논 감정

수박은 가게에 쌓여서도 익지요
익다 못해 늙지요
검은 줄무늬에 갇혀
수박은
속은 타서 붉고 씨는 검고
말은 안 하지요 결국 못 하지요
그걸
레바논 감정이라 할까 봐요

나귀가 수박을 싣고 갔어요
방울을 절렁이며 타클라마칸 사막 오아시스
백양나무 가로수 사이로 거긴 아직도
나귀가 교통수단이지요
시장엔 은반지 금반지 세공사들이
무언가 되고 싶어 엎드려 있지요

될 수 없는 무엇이 되고 싶어
그들은 거기서 나는 여기서 죽지요
그들은 거기서 살았고 나는 여기서 살았지요
살았던가요, 나? 사막에서?
레바논에서?

폭탄 구멍 뚫린 집들을 배경으로
베일 쓴 여자들이 지나가지요
퀭한 눈을 번득이며 오락가락 갈매기처럼
그게 바로 나였는지도 모르지요

When, instead of a reply,
I got my letter back, torn to pieces,
it was like a dream,
I thought it could not be.
But can that be called Lebanese emotion too?

All over the world, lovers become ex-lovers.
The man returns home in full glory, riding in glimmering cars.
He goes to Lebanon to be a king.
He goes to Lebanon to speak a foreign language and marry again.

He becomes a father and flashes a quick smile.
White teeth behind black lips,
why doesn't he die?
And when he does why won't he just go away?

He blows in like a wind from across the desert,
a wind almost forgotten, clouds aloft with his breath.
The clouds float up, they drift along,
they cry red.
They hold their heads in their hands and whimper.
They glance off to the side, and, finally,

today, it rains all day.
Shall I call it Lebanese emotion?
Shall I call these Lebanese clouds?
Rising and falling—
let's call it Lebanon. Yes, let's do that.

내가 쓴 편지가 갈가리 찢겨져
답장 대신 돌아왔을 때
꿈만 같아서
그 때는 현실이 아니라고 우겼는데
그것도 레바논 감정이라 할까요?

세상의 모든 애인은 옛애인이 되지요*
옛애인은 다 금의환향하고 옛애인은 번쩍이는 차를 타고
옛애인은 레바논으로 가 왕이 되지요
레바논으로 가 외국어로 떠들고 또 결혼을 하지요

옛애인은 아빠가 되고 옛애인은 씨익 웃지요
검은 입술에 하얀 이빨
옛애인들은 왜 죽지 않는 걸까요
죽어도 왜 흐르지 않는 걸까요

사막 건너에서 바람처럼 불어 오지요
잊을 만하면 바람은 구름을 불러 띄우지요
구름은 뜨고 구름은 흐르고 구름은 붉게 울지요
얼굴을 감싸 쥐고 징징거리다
눈을 흘기고 결국

오늘은 종일 비가 왔어요
그걸 레바논 감정이라 할까 봐요
그걸 레바논 구름이라 할까 봐요
떴다 내리는
그걸 레바논이라 합시다 그립시다

* 박정대의 시에서

CRIMSON FIELD

I must have dozed off for a second. Riding the train, I saw a crimson field among green valleys. The furrows curved softly. Strangely, there wasn't a single blade of grass. And then it was gone. It was just for a moment. I've never seen it again, although I watch attentively every time I pass that place.

I don't remember why. Mother stuffed my school books into the small opening of our *agung'i*. What good will school do you? I raked the books out—their pages warped and burned—packed them up, and took them to school for one semester. I don't know why.

I don't remember what I did with my half-burned school bag. I have no idea where the field went, or why it decided it would not push up even a single blade of grass. Sometimes, when I wake in the middle of the night, I find myself lying in that crimson field.

붉은 밭

　　깜빡 잠이 들었었나 봅니다 기차를 타고 가다가 푸른 골짜기 사이 붉은 밭 보았습니다 고랑 따라 부드럽게 구불거리고 있었습니다 이상하게 풀 한포기 없었습니다 그러곤 사라졌습니다 잠깐이었습니다 거길 지날 때마다 유심히 살폈는데 그 밭 다시 볼 수 없었습니다

무슨 일 때문인지는 기억나지 않습니다 엄마가 내 교과서를 이궁이에 쳐넣었습니다 학교같은 건 다녀 뭐하냐고 했습니다 나는 아궁이를 뒤져 가장자리가 검게 구불거리는 책을 싸들고 한학기 동안 학교에 다녔습니다 왜 그랬는지 모릅니다

타다만 책가방 그후 어찌했는지 기억나지 않습니다 그 밭 왜 풀 한포기 내밀지 않기로 작정했는지 그러다가 어디로 사라졌는지 알 수 없습니다 가끔 한밤중에 깨어보면 내가 붉은 밭에 누워 있기도 했습니다

IN FRONT OF MY OLD HOUSE

The house is carrying a wardrobe.
The wardrobe is carrying a coat,
and the coat is carrying me.

The time jolts forward.
The trees standing along the street gradually run away,
and birds fly off like curses.

Without knowing anything,
lava is boiling underground,
animals copulate,
and seeds suddenly rot.

A flood happens, and time floats on the muddy water.
Inside the wardrobe, inside the coat, inside a headache

I was the trap
from which I couldn't escape.

The headache throws me away,
the coat breaks the wardrobe,
the wardrobe betrays the house.

I pass that unfamiliar old house like a ghost.
The forgotten spring
goes away like a sour taste.

옛집 앞을

그 집은 장롱을 안고 있다
장롱은 외투를 외투는 나를 안고 있다

덜컹거리며 흘러간다
길가에 나무들 서서히 달아나고
욕설을 퍼붓듯 새들이 날아간다

아무것도 모르고
지하에서 용암은 끓고 있다
짐승들은 교미하고
씨앗은 갑자기 썩는다

홍수가 나고 붉은 시간의 흙탕
위를 떠다닌다
장롱 속에 외투 속에 두통 속에

바로 내가
붙잡을 수 없는 덫이었다

두통이 나를 팽개친다
외투가 장롱을 부숴버린다
장롱이 그집을 저버린다

낯선 옛집 앞을 유령처럼 흘러간다
잊어버린 봄이 신맛처럼 지나간다

RED MARBLE

I wore a school uniform. I cried, hunched over. I was a high school senior and my name was Yi Hong-ju. My younger brother lay dying by the sliding door. Looking inside, you could see a one-room house with a small kitchen, you could see the coal furnace and, putting your shoes beside it, could enter over the wooden planks of a little vestibule. The door was closed; I sobbed with my face to the cold floor. I woke shaking to that sound.

There is a police box beside the road I walk every day. A wreath of peonies is suddenly hanging in front of it. The buds tremble as each car passes by. Soon they are covered with dust, and wither.

Hong-ju? I've never seen or heard the name. I don't know the little brother that died. A long time has passed since I've been the mother of two; I lounge in an apartment with four rooms. You say I'm a high school girl named Hong-ju? Dressed in a school uniform, crying in a small vestibule.

Strange. Like being trapped in a red marble. I walk by the police box without knowing anything. Suddenly, a blood-colored marble that isn't my name, and peonies, hardly trying to bloom, covered in dust.

붉은 구슬

교복을 입고 있었다 엎드려 울고 있었다 내 이름은 이 홍주라고 했고 고3
이었다 미닫이 문 저쪽엔 어린 동생이 죽어 누워 있었다 방 하나에 부엌이
딸린 집 문을 열면 연탄 아궁이가 보이고 아궁이 옆에 신발을 벗어놓고
쪽마루를 디뎌야 방으로 들어갈 수 있었다 방문은 닫혀 있고 찬 바닥에
얼굴을 대고 흐느껴 울었다 울음소리에 흔들려 깨어났다

매일 지나다니는 길 옆에는 파출소가 있다 파출소 앞에 갑자기 모란이
한무더기 매달렸다 차들이 지날 때마다 모란 꽃송이가 부르르 떨었다 곧
먼지에 덮였다 졌다

홍주라니 듣도 보도 못한 이름이었다 그 집 죽은 동생 기억에 없다 두 아이의
엄마가 된게 언제인데 방이 넷인 아파트에서 이렇게 누워 있는데 내가 교복을
입고 쪽마루에 엎드려 우는 고등학생 홍주라니

이상하다 붉은 구슬 속에 갇힌 것 같다 아무것도 모르고 파출소 앞을 내가
지나다닌다 갑자기 매달린 모란 봉오리 내 이름이 아닌 핏빛 구슬 덩어리
좀처럼 피려 않던 먼지에 덮인

INTENT ON FORGETTING THE BODY

Opium poppies swayed in the turtle's eyes;
Nakhwa Crags had three-thousand palace girls by its side.

The cat lives beneath the car tire,
the cancer cell beneath the rib,
meowing. Meowing.

When, across from the hospital
far from here,
trains cross the Han,
when they jerk and wriggle across
like cabbage worms,

the snowstorm in the mustard seed,
the distant hill in the cuckoos' cries—

everything is intent on forgetting the body
and the smell of this world,

In the eyelid, into the daydream,
beneath the bluff, the cherry blossoms,
everything floats, scattered and aloft.

온몸을 잊으려고

양귀비는 거북 눈 속에서 하늘거리고
낙화암은 옆구리에 삼천궁녀를 거느렸네

차바퀴 밑에는 고양이가
늑골 아래에는 암세포가
야옹거리며 야옹거리며 사네

종합병원 건너편 저 멀리에
기차가 한강 다리를 건널 때
초록 배추벌레처럼
꿈틀거리며 꿈틀거리며 건널 때

겨자씨 속엔 눈폭풍이
뻐꾹소리 속엔 먼 산이

온몸을 잊으려고
이 세상 냄새를 잊으려고

눈꺼풀 속으로 백일몽 속으로
절벽 아래로 벚꽃잎 아래로
흩날리네 흩날리네

A MEAL AT THE AQUARIUM RESTAURANT

He looked down on me and, coming close, opened his mouth.
We had parted long ago in the plains of the big sea
but were brought, caught, to this aquarium restaurant, which is green
    in every direction.

I started picking moss from boulders a while ago too
and chewing, in little bites, the baby fish.
Your eyes were the eyes of that old turtle from two-hundred years ago,
the blue eyes of the shark from one-hundred years ago,
and now, again, the eyes of that quiet bream.
Addicted to your look, my teeth chattered.

When they rose from the abyss and came for me,
I wanted to look into the bottom of myself,
this groundless *here*—
neither day nor night—
this *here* that's not on land or at sea,
like seaweed swept aside by a tidal wave, it came,
this tangle: and who are all of you?
Twisted body, fins slapping, mouth open,
following one-hundred-year-old, two-hundred-year-old teeth and
    tongues, a liver and
gills,
the screaming waves folding over and coming like shot arrows
to crash and spill out inside of me—the *me* inside of me,
having wandered off so frequently, I wanted to throw it away.

수족관 식당에서의 식사

그는 나를 굽어보고 다가와서 입을 벌렸지요
오래 전에 큰바다 벌판에서 작별을 고하고
사방 푸른 이 수족관 식당에 들어와 갇히게 되었다고

나도 바위 이끼를 뜯고 이빨에 고기 새끼를 끼워
잘게 잘게 씹고 있는지 오래
당신의 눈은 200년 전부터 늙은 거북의 눈
100년 전부터는 푸른 상어의 눈
그러다가 이제는 다시 고요한 도미의 눈
그 빛에 중독되어 내 이빨도 덜그럭거렸지요

그들이 심연에서 떠올라 내게로 다가올 때
나도 나 자신을 밑바닥까지 보고 싶었어요
이 터무니없는 낮도 밤도 아닌 여기
땅 속도 바다속도 아닌 여기
해일에 미역줄기처럼 떠밀려왔다가 엉켜버리는
이것들은 다 누구인지

몸을 비틀어 꼬리를 치고 턱뼈를 벌려
100년 된 200년 된 이빨과 혓바닥을 간과 허파를
쏜살같이 달려와 뒤집히며 깔깔거리는 파도를 따라
엎어지고 쏟아뜨려 내 속에 내 속에
수백 번 헤매다닌 나를 팽개치고 싶었어요

The baby fish, waving their fins, will be returning from school.
Swaying on clamorous waves,
are you the baby bream coming here from somewhere? Are you
    seaweed headed
someplace?
In curiosity, they turn back, their eyes jiggle and look around—

And, in the end, we'll be swallowed up.
When the tsunami between passes between you and me
and my house on the hill is submerged,
every dog in the country will bark and,
every time we look back,
the moon will scorn the high wave of emotion
that chases at our heels.
Looking down at my house underwater,
sitting in an easy chair, between clouds.

새끼고기들은 꼬리치며 학교에서 돌아오겠지요
왁자지껄 물결에 흔들리며
어디서 온 도미새끼이냐 어디로 가는 미역줄기냐
호기심에 흔들리다 뒤돌아서 눈알을 궁글리고

아무래도 삼켜지고 말겠지요
당신과 나 사이에 이 해일이 끝나면
산중턱 내 집은 물에 잠기고
온 나라의 개들은 컹컹 짖고
돌아볼 때마다 우리 발꿈치를 좇아오던
감정의 이 높은 파도를
달은 비웃겠지요
물에 잠긴 내 집을 내려다보며
구름 사이 안락의자에 앉아서

A SWAMP AND A POEM

Don't go there, you keep saying.
Don't fall in, you say.
But I end up going, you see.
I hesitate,
but, in the end,
I crawl through the dark hole. Crawl.
No way not to.
The houses there
have collapsed;
their shadows are lying down.
The river water has already flowed by,
and the hills, the temples, the food, the poems
lie there thin, passing time.
I hide and cry, you see,
digging up shadows,
becoming a shadow,
and scampering like a mouse.

Even if I escape somehow,
there's no being
a farmer
a *kwangdae*
a tradesman.
You see, I can't even keep living meanly.

늪과 시

그곳엔 가지 말라고들 하지
빠지지 말라고도 하지
그러나 가게 된다지
망설이다 결국은
깜깜한 구멍을 기어서 기어서
부득불 간다지
그곳은
집은 무너지고
집의 그림자만 누워 있다지
강물은 이미 흘러가 버렸고
산도 절도 밥도 시도
얇게 누워 지낸다지
숨어서 울게 된다지
그림자만 퍼먹게 된다지
그림자가 되어
쥐처럼 기어다닌다지

어쩌다 빠져나온다 해도
그 다음엔
농사를 지을 수도
광대가 될 수도
장사를 할 수도 없다지
비굴하게나마 살아갈 수가 없다지

TIGERS IN THE SUNLIGHT

I am standing with my arms up
or hugging a bomb that's heating up.

Straight upright and motionless, I glare, my eyes transfixed—tiger's
    eyes, not yellow, not
flaming red, but a burning green behind stiff whiskers.

Sunlight spills brightly over everything;
from the asphalt's painfully quiet scream.

*

I glared out. Great-grandmother met a tiger in a sloping field. It's
women who make a house. Her head sizzled; the stony field crackled.
The tiger's eyes blazed so much that it turned and slipped out of sight.
Yes, so, the young calf—her whole inheritance—was protected.
Grandmother's tears tumbled out over the stony field. Buds appeared
and leaves sprouted.

*

Today I meet the tiger and it says,
"I won't kill you if you give me a rice cake."

No matter how hard I stare at the traffic light, still all jammed up.

"Give me one leg!
Give me one arm!"

햇빛 속에 호랑이

나는 지금 두 손 들고 서 있는 거라
뜨거운 폭탄을 안고 있는 거라

부동자세로 두 눈 부릅뜨고 노려보고 있는 거라 빠빳한 수염털 사이로 노랑
　　이그르한 빨강 아니 불타는 초록의 호랑이 눈깔을

햇빛은 광광 내리 퍼붓고
아스팔트 너무나 고요한 비명 속에서

노려보고 있었던 거라, 증조 할머니 비탈밭에서 호랑이를 만나, 결국 집안을
일으킨 건 여자들인 거라, 머리가 지글거리고 돌밭이 지글거리고, 호랑이 눈깔
타들어가다 못해 슬몃 뒤돌아 가버렸던 거라. 그래 전재산이었던 엇송아지를
지켰고, 할머니 눈물 돌밭에 굴러 싹이 나고 잎이 나고

그러다가 떡 하나 주면 안 잡아먹지 하는
식의 호랑이를 만난 것이라

신호등을 아무리 노려봐도 꽉 막혀서

- 다리 한 짝 떼어 놓으시지
- 팔도 한 짝 떼어 놓으시지

Even though I say don't have any, don't have any, don't have any
and say I'm not my great-grandmother...

"Give me your head, your heart, your kidney, won't you?
And your guts, please!"

The sunlight is fierce—
oh, those little tigers swarming in it.

이젠 없다 없다 없다는데도
나는 증조할머니가 아니라 해도

— 머리통 염통 콩팥 다 내 놓으시지
— 내장도 마저 꺼내 놓으시지

저 햇빛 사나와 햇빛 속에 우글우글
아이구 저 호랑이 새끼들

I TALKED WITH GEESE IN IOWA

Returning from the rodeo in the van
I'm beginning to doze.
A little fluffy dog is coming towards me.
As soon as I begin to murmur in my mother tongue,
"What's with you, little dog?"
the puppy turns into a water bottle.

Whenever I open my mouth,
my words change to an alien's.
The more eagerly I express my thoughts,
the stranger my words become.

Walking beside the river
I meet some geese.
They quack-quack—
the same as Korean geese.

I step up to them;
they do not run away, but peck my foot,
knowing nothing but quack-quack
as that is their mother tongue.
There is no more arrogant answer.

거위와 말했다

- 아이오와에서

로데오 구경하고 돌아오는데
버스에서 잠깐 졸았다
조그만 털강아지가 내품으로 달겨들고 있었다
웬 강아지냐고
우리 말로 잠꼬대를 하는 순간
털강아지는 다시 물병으로 변해 버렸다.

우리말이 통할 리 없는 여기
입을 열면 외계인이 먼저 말을 한다
생각이 열렬할수록
말은 주문이 된다

강변을 걷다가
거위와 만났다
거위는 꽥꽥 소리쳤다
한국 거위 울음소리와 똑같았다

반가와서 다가섰더니
내발을 콕콕 찍는 것이다
꽥꽥 그 말밖에 모르면서
그것도 자기네 말이라고
그지없이 건방진 대답을 하는 것이다

SMELL

The smell escapes from itself
and looks at its body for a long time.

Without revealing its wings
or the sound of their flapping,
it's the bird the body lets fly out.

Smell is the guide
for the underworld of the thick darkness.

I just baked a mackerel.
The whole house smells.
It hovers
over the kids doing their arithmetic,
and over me, doing the dishes.

I open a window to shoo it away
but it sneaks into the cracks of the dresser drawers and the chink to hide.
It's so quiet.
It's so stubborn.
It won't show the tips of its extended wings after all.

A lead-gray belly blinks as it crosses the ocean—
smell, in the end, flies off.

A coal-like lump flies out
beyond the evening lights.
A dark sky is not far away,
stiffening.

냄 새

냄새가 자신을 빠져나와
한참 동안 제 몸을 들여다 보고 있다

날개도 날개치는 소리도
보여주지 않는
냄새는 육신이 날리는 새다

딱딱한 지하를 헤치고 날아갈
어둠의 앞잡이다

고등어 한 마리를 구워 먹었는데
온 집안에 냄새다
산수 숙제를 하는 애들에게서
설거지를 하는 내게서 냄새가
가지 않고 머뭇거린다

냄새를 쫓으려고 창문을 열어도
냄새는 옷장 속으로 문틈으로 숨는다
냄새는 조용하다
냄새는 악착같다
펼친 날개는 끝내 보여주지 않는다

납빛 배를 번쩍이며 해협을 누비던 것처럼
그러나 냄새는 결국 날아간다

저녁 불빛 밖으로
이제 막 날아가는 숯덩이같은 게 있다
멀지 않은 곳에 검은 하늘이 있다
딱딱하게 굳은

PYŎNGJŎM

In Pyŏngjŏm there is a small train station. My father, a railway worker, comes walking on the black gravel. Beside the railway, flower upon flower of cockscomb. Somewhere the cry of a rooster. Pyŏngjŏm had a rice cake shop. When my mother was pregnant with me and had morning sickness, she ripped off a small part of the rice cake and ate it at the shop. She ate it again after setting down a sack of beans from the top of her head. My flesh is a part of that Pyŏngjŏm rice cake. Pyŏngjŏm is my flesh. Cockscombs beside the railway were me, my sister, and my brother. When the Saemaŭl express train passed them, shabby cockscombs were surprised and fell down. Now there is no rice cake shop in Pyŏngjŏm. My sister is dead. And the road splits off toward Suwŏn, Osan, and Chŏngnam, stretching away, endlessly.

餠店

　　병점엔 조그만 기차역 있다 검은 자갈돌 밟고 철도원 아버지 걸어 오신다
철길가에 맨드라미 맨드라미 있었다 어디서 얼룩 수탉 울었다 병점엔 떡집 있었다
우리 어머니 날 배고 입덧 심할 때 병점 떡집서 떡 한점 떼어 먹었다 머리에 인
콩 한 자루 내려 놓고 또 한점 떼어 먹었다 내 살은 병점 떡 한점이다 병점은 내
살점이다 병점 철길가에 맨드라미는 나다 내 언니다 내 동생이다 새마을 특급
열차가 지나갈 때 꾀죄죄한 맨드라미 깜짝 놀라 자빠졌다 지금 병점엔 떡집 없다
우리 언니는 죽었고 水原, 烏山, 正南으로 가는 길은 여기서 헤어져 끝없이 갔다

CRABS WITH ONE LEG INSIDE THEIR HOLES

Little crabs scuttling over the mud flat
stop, suddenly,
in unison,
as if receiving a command from their Creator.

I have no plans, none.
Not even to break off some legs
to steam and eat.

Even so,
startled by my presence
as they scamper along,
they've raised their antennae high
to watch from across the flats.
Pretending to watch the flats, they watch me watching them instead.

The hibiscus has blossomed—
like that game,
when suddenly, to avoid me,
they move in unison and with such speed
that the horizon seems to spin
in the many moments of their crab-steps.

I'm dizzy.
The sky has been flipped onto the mudflat, the sea into the sky.

I stand on the breakwater enjoying the air,
just the flapping of my coat.

I feel sorry
when the crabs live, pretending to be dead,
one leg inside their holes, looking at me.

게들은 구멍 속에 한 쪽 다리를 걸치고

갯벌에 꼬물대던 작은 게들이
갑자기
천지 개벽의 지령이라도 받은 것처럼
일제히 정지한다

나는 아무런 의도가 없어, 없어
너희를 잡아 다리를 부러뜨릴 생각도
찜쪄 먹을 계획도 없다구

그래도
꼬물거리던 그들은 내 기척에
기겁을 하고
눈의 안테나를 높이 세우고
뻘 저편을 바라본다
바라보는 척 게눈 뜨고 내 눈치를 본다

무궁화꽃이 피었습니다
놀이처럼
그들이 내 발길을 피해
일제히 재빠르게 몸을 옮길 때
순간의 무수한 게걸음에
수평선이 빙그르 도는 것 같다

아찔하다
하늘은 뻘로 바다는 하늘로 뒤집힌다

난 바람을 쐬러 방파제에 서 있고
옷자락이 펄럭일 뿐인데

섭섭하다
게들이 구멍 속에 한쪽 다리를 걸치고
죽은 척 살아서 내 눈치를 볼 때

WHEN I WAS TREMBLING LIKE A LEAF

My grandfather died twenty-five years ago.
Fifty-five years before that time
there was a Kamulch'i cooking on a fireplace.
My family sat around a table,
ate the soup, saying that the flesh
made it delicious;
they emptied each bowl.

My grandmother died thirty-five years ago.
Forty-five years before that time
the Kamulch'i they forgot to put in the cauldron
was left cooking on the fireplace.
My family ate the soup without Kamulch'i,
they finished each bowl, saying
that it was special
because of the flesh in it.

My father hid himself in a cave during the Korean War.
Thirty-five years before the war
my father was a child.
Inside him, I was much smaller than a particle.
That instant, I saw a Kamulch'i on a cooking fireplace
and I as a little particle went into the body of the soup.

And one hundred years before then,
my grand-Kamulch'i experienced a big drought.
The bottom of the river broke and he wriggled.
He breathed with a mouth instead of gills
and then jumped ashore.
My family killed and ate each other to live.
Finally some wriggled and died.

내가 한 잎 나뭇잎이었을 때

25년 전 할아버지가 죽었다
할아버지가 죽은 해로부터 다시 55년 전
부뚜막에는 가물치가 있었다
할아버지 할머니 아버지 고모 삼촌 들
둘러앉아 가물치 국을 먹었다
역시 남의 살이 들어가니 맛있다며 한 대접씩 마셨다

35년 전 할머니가 죽었다
할머니가 죽은 해로부터 다시 45년 전
부뚜막에는 가물치가 아직 있었다
깜빡 잊고 솥에 들어 가지 못한 가물치가 있었다
식구들은 가물치 빠진 헛가물치 국을 마시고
역시 남의 살이 들어 가니 다르다며 한 대접씩 먹었다

45년전 아버지는 전쟁을 만나 동굴 속에 숨어 있었다
그로부터 다시 35년전 아버지는 아이였다
조그만 아버지 속의 더 작은
나는 부뚜막 위 가물치를 보았고
나는 가물치 속으로 들어가고 말았다

내가 한마리 가물치 속에 있을 때로부터 다시 100년 전
나의 할아버지 가물치는 큰 가뭄을 만났다
강바닥이 갈라져 몸부림쳤다
아가미 대신 입으로 숨쉬다 땅에 올랐다
살려고 식구끼리 잡아 먹었다
결국은 몸 비틀고 죽기도 했다

One hundred years before my grand-Kamulch'i's death,
the surviving Kamulch'i climbed up the trees every night.
As in the old tale
of how the moon rose and the stars rose,
they climbed up the trees.
Those tired trees standing along the dried-up river!
I who was in the Kamulch'i shook
their arms out endlessly
shaking my black backbone
and spreading my fishy smell,
I turned myself into a leaf and fluttered in the wind.

When I was trembling like a leaf
one hundred eighty years ago, and again two hundred years before that,
I seemed to see and hear
leaves that were green withered suddenly;
everlasting holidays came unexpectedly;
I seemed to see this moment today, like a sinking ship,
I saw a strange version of myself there.

할아버지 가물치가 죽은 해로부터 다시 100년 전
밤이면 살아남은 가물치 나무에 올랐다
달이 떠오르다 별이 뜨다 라는 아득한 말처럼
나무에 기어 올랐다

마른 강줄기를 따라선 지친 나무들
하염없이 두 팔 벌린 그들 가슴을
가물치 속의 내가 흔들었다
검은 등줄기로 툭툭 치면서
비린내를 풍기면서
몸 바꿔 나뭇잎으로 펄럭였다

180년 전 그로부터 다시 200년 전
내가 한 잎 나뭇잎으로 흔들릴 때
본 것 같았다 들은 것 같았다
푸르렀던 것 갑자기 시들어지고
문득 영원한 휴일이 오고
뜻도없이 침몰하는 배 한 척
오늘 이 순간에 타고 있는 이상한 나를 본 것만 같았다

FROG! GRASSHOPPER! DUNG BEETLE!

Hey—frog!
Grasshopper! Springing up like fried peas and beans
with all your might!
Dung beetle! with the force of your love.
Let's go on
rolling the horseshit,
falling into it.
You—Frog. Grasshopper. Dung beetle!
Across that field, over that roof!
Even if you close the gate and lock yourself away at home,
you'll be suddenly slapped on the cheek and cursed at.
Repaying our debts, we repay our debts,
until leaves and shoots sprout in the barbed wire,
flowers bloom and flowers fall
until watermelons hang from the chestnut trees in big bunches,
until the peach and apricot pits go on a rampage,
let's go.
Shove the horseshit, push it!
Uh… Frog! Grasshopper! Dung beetle!
Let's head over there,
rolling our horseshit, the bullshit,
in the world, out of the world, for the successful world.

개구리 메뚜기 말똥구리야

너 개구리야
그 힘으로
콩튀듯 팥튀듯 뛰는 메뚜기야
네 사랑의 힘으로 말똥구리야
우리 말똥을 굴리며
엎어지며 고꾸라지며 가자
저 들판을 지붕을 건너
개구리 메뚜기 말똥구리야
대문 걸어 잠그고 두문불출한다해도
느닷없이 따귀 맞고 욕설은 듣게 된다
빚 갚고 갚으며
철조망에 싹이 나고 잎이 날 때까지
꽃 피고 꽃 지고
밤나무에 주렁주렁 수박덩이가 매달릴 때까지
복사씨도 살구씨도 미쳐 날뛸 때까지*
가자
말똥을 굴리며 굴리며
으으 개구리 메뚜기 말똥구리야
세간에 세간에 출세 간에
그 너머로 우리
말똥을 소똥을 굴리며 가자

* 김수영 시 〈사랑의 變奏曲〉에서

AN ARROW LYING ON THE ROAD

Your plane takes off

and, about now, will be in the clouds.
It'll be floating over the ocean.
It will touch down eventually.

But I try not to think about it.
Instead, I let the clouds of your breath know

that there are green apples and red apples,
that the green apples and the red apples
are cheek-to-cheek at the roadside stall,

that a truck passes in front of me,
that the thick leeks, stacked high like books, are tied with rope in the truck
that they are tied, root to root, stalk to stalk,
each to the other, fastened together so tightly that they,
tied like that, have not a gap anywhere between them.

In the sky's blank notebook,
I write that I want to drink
all the apples of an apple tree.

I drink an apple tree
and ask the arrow on the road

Now is it in the clouds? Over the ocean? Touching down?

I write that I'll follow the white arrow bending left.
That hope behaves outrageously
so, every day, chased by it, I go a little farther.

길에 누운 화살표

네 비행기 날아가고

지금쯤 구름 속에 있겠다
바다 위에 떴겠다
드디어 땅바닥에 닿았겠다

그러나 생각 않기로 한다
대신 네 호흡인 구름에게

푸른 사과와 붉은 사과가 있다고 전한다
좌판에 푸른 사과와 붉은 사과가
서로의 볼을 맞대고 있다고

내 앞에 트럭이 지나간다고
굵은 대파가 책처럼 높다랗게 쌓였고 밧줄에 묶였고
뿌리는 뿌리끼리 푸른 잎은 잎끼리
서로가 서로를 꽉 채우고 빈틈 하나 없이 저렇게
묶여 실려 간다고

허공 속의 공책에
사과를 사과나무를
다 마셔버리고 싶다고 쓴다

사과나무 한 채를 다 마시고
지금쯤은 구름 속인지 바다 위인지 땅바닥인지

길바닥에 누운 화살표에게 묻는다

좌로 꺾인 하얀 화살표 따라 간다고 쓴다
희망은 난폭해서
날마다 쫓기며 가보게 한다고

Do you think dolphins can live in a river? I have never thought that to be possible; yet, an incredible thing happened in Seoul, Korea. Surprisingly, last April, a dead dolphin was found on the riverbank near the Panp'o Bridge of Seoul's Han River. The Han River is very wide and deep, but sluggish; the water is not clean enough for dolphins to live in it.

Then why did he go against the stream? Why did he want to leave the West Sea and swim up the Han River? Was he looking for his ancestors who moved from land to sea a long time ago? There would have been many obstacles for him, such as sluice gates, a dam under construction, and many noisy railroad bridges. And above all, the fresh water, unlike his native seawater, could have tormented him terribly. Moreover, how could he swim over the dam? I guess the high tide made it possible for him to jump into the river. He would have suffered increasingly from the lowering salt content in the water. The dolphin would have tried to go back to the sea, but maybe he could not find the direction because his pain was too severe to generate sonar waves. Later, an investigator announced that it was a kind of harbor porpoise. He found a big, festering wound inside the stomach, and it seemed like the dolphin had indeed had difficulty using his sonar waves.

Like a dolphin, sometimes I lose my sense of direction and time. I don't know where I am and when is now. Whenever these strange times happen, it's like my sonar waves won't work. I have an illusion; I mistake a flying stone for a bird. (I have thrown stones a few times in anti-government demonstrations in the 1970s and 80s.) These moments are usually short, but sometimes they last long enough to build a kingdom. These moments inspire me to write poems, such as this one: [see "In Three Minutes," p. 20]

I wander in an illusion of these moments. Whenever I ask myself who I am and what I'm doing, I cannot help but recall my past. Memories shimmer in my mind and remind me how I've become what I am. In one memory: [see "Crimson Field," p. 102]

These memories are scattered inside me, and they wander in the mist of time. In the fragments of memories, I feel like I can find my real existence, and I think it is the way I understand the world and others. As you can tell from my poems, memory is both my deficiency and my mind's ruin. I wanted to escape these moments of deficiency and ruin to reach this world. That is, I wanted to understand the pain of others, and eventually the whole world, by way of my own pain.

Let me go back to the dolphin story. Why did the dolphin leave the sea and swim up the river? Why did it desire to go elsewhere? The answer to this question is the same as the reason why I began to write. I wanted to leave the place where I had lived—to dare to swim against the times or to go to a new place. And that also brings me here now. But here, in Iowa, my sonar waves won't work; my native language became useless. Here, I think of my language and my country. Korea is a very small country geographically; moreover, it is divided into north and south.

Many Koreans, including myself, still suffer from memories of the Korean War in the 50s, the division and the poverty we experienced. These days when I watch bombs exploding in a poor country on TV, it reminds me of my childhood. I also grew up eating candy, chocolates, and gum that the American soldiers threw to us along the railroad tracks. We, the poor, were hurt by the insolence and pride hidden inside the kindness of the rich. When I was young, I used to wish that I had been born in a rich country. However, come to think of it, I think I love my country because it is small and because it suffered so much in its history. Remembering the hurt is not only the willingness to recover from it, but also an effort to prevent hurting others. If I had grown up in a wealthy country, I would have enjoyed life more, wasting time and energy, drinking, dancing, and so on. Of course, I would never have tried to write poetry to remember the pain.

In Iowa, my mother-tongue is useless. Here, a Korean writer, Pak Kyŏng-ni, comes to mind. She devoted twenty-four years to finishing a single novel (which is in sixteen volumes). I love her passion for and persistence in her career. Her novel, *Land*, opens in 1897, a turbulent time when Korean people were struggling against their history. She once said, "I didn't know how to write this novel. It was like someone else was writing it through me. If I had not been unhappy, I would not have written *Land* for such a long time—twenty-four years for one novel!"

Many Korean people think Pak Kyŏng-ni's novel could be loved by the whole world. But there are too many references to Korean customs and too many Korean idioms to translate it easily. I love her novel and admire the full twenty-four years she dedicated to it. I admire her language that digs deep into the human mind and into our sad history. I write in a language that is internationally less prominent than other languages. My language becomes useless when I go abroad. Whenever I think it is useless, I think of Pak Kyŏng-ni and her dedication of twenty-four years. Difficulty of communication doesn't mean a language has no worth or depth.

But I didn't answer why I write yet, or if, like Pak Kyŏng-ni, I write because I'm unhappy—maybe; maybe not. We live only once; this is frustrating. So we have to do our best in our time. I think that is my duty and a courtesy. Someone gave me life and I should answer. Now that I am alive and have a memory and can feel things deeply, I have to answer the questions of who I am, and where I am. So I write.

Jeongrye Choi
Written in English in Iowa City, 2006

NOTES

Motes — *Sundubu* is a tofu soup.

The Airplane Took Off. The Airplane Disappeared. — The poem by Miguel Hernández is "Vuelo (Flight)."

Deer Climbing a Bamboo Pole — The poem incorporates elements from a number of Korea's creation myths, which feature deer and miraculous human births from eggs. The *haegŭm* is a fiddle-like instrument. *Yalli yalli yallangsŏng / yallari yalla* . . . is a meaningless refrain from the Koryŏ dynasty (935 – 1392) folk song, "Ch'ŏngsan pyŏlgok (Song of Green Hills)," first recorded during the early Chosŏn dynasty (1392 – 1910).

Canna and the Sword — "Flower cards" is a very literal translation of *hwat'u*, which is a card game.

Her Lips are Warm While Yours are Cold — The poem refers to the 1946 pop song "Release Me" by Eddie Miller, Robert Yount, and Dub Williams; the lyrics quoted have been translated into Korean and back into English.

The Evening's Supermarket — "My cousin bought some land, and my stomach hurts" is an idiomatic expression of jealousy.

Red Tubs — *Yŏt* is a kind of taffy made from grain or potatoes.

An Apple Seller Scattered in Front of a Musso — A Musso is an SUV made by Ssangyong.

Blood — The noun for "blood (*p'i*, 피)" and the verb "to blossom (*p'ida*, 피다)" are homophones; Choi plays with this throughout the poem. *Kiyŏk* refers to "ㄱ," the first letter of the Korean alphabet.

Crimson Field — *Agung'i* is a type of furnace with a small opening for wood in front and a cast iron pot on top, where meals in a house like this would have been cooked. This "furnace/hearth fire/kitchen stove" would be used, through a series of flues running from it through the rest of the house, to heat the floors.

Red Marble — "Hong-ju" means "red marble."

Intent on Forgetting the Body — Nakhwa Crags is a bluff in South Ch'ungch'ŏng Province where, according to legend, 3,000 palace women jumped to their deaths following the fall of the Korean kingdom of Paekche to another Korean kingdom, Silla, in 660. "The Han" is the Han River.

A Swamp and a Poem — None of *kwangdae*'s standard translations (singer, clown, jester, acrobat) sufficiently describe the various roles these performers undertake. Some are singers of Korea's operatic art *p'ansori*, while others are similar to slap-stick comedians. For a history and detailed explanation of the *kwangdae*'s place in Korea's performative traditions see Marshall R. Pihl's *The Korean Singer of Tales*.

TIGERS IN THE SUNLIGHT — The poem plays with a Korean fairytale about a tiger that eats the mother of two children when she runs out of the rice cakes the tiger demands.

I TALKED WITH GEESE IN IOWA — The poem was originally written in English in Iowa City and then later rewritten in Korean.

SMELL — Plays on "*sae* (새, bird)" and "*naemsae* (냄새, smell)" guide the metaphors in this poem.

PYŎNGJŎM — "Pyŏngjŏm" means "rice-cake shop" and is the name of the author's hometown. The poem has been translated by Choi Jongyoll, with modifications by the author.

CRABS WITH ONE LEG INSIDE THEIR HOLES — "The hibiscus has blossomed" is a children's game similar to "freeze tag." One person covering their eyes recites, "The hibiscus flowers have blossomed 무궁화 꽃이 피었습니다." While the phrase is being recited, everyone else playing runs to tag the person reciting the phrase. Once the phrase has been completed, everyone must freeze in place until the phrase is recited again.

WHEN I WAS TREMBLING AS A LEAF — "Kamulch'i" is the name of a fish similar to a mullet or snakehead; a fish caught during a drought, when the water is low. The poem has been translated by Choi Jongyoll and Jordan Stempelman, with modifications by the author.

FROG! GRASSHOPPER! DUNG BEETLE! — The line "until the peach and apricot pits go on a rampage" is from Kim Su-yŏng's (1921-1968) poem "Variations on Love." Kim is a central figure of twentieth-century Korean literature.

FREE VERSE EDITIONS

Edited by Jon Thompson

13 ways of happily by Emily Carr
A Map of Faring by Peter Riley
An Unchanging Blue: Selected Poems 1962-1975 by
      Rolf Dieter Brinkmann, translated by Mark Terrill
Between the Twilight and the Sky by Jennie Neighbors
Blood Orbits by Ger Killeen
Child in the Road by Cindy Savett
Current by Lisa Fishman
Divination Machine by F. Daniel Rzicznek
Physis by Nicolas Pesque, translated by Cole Swensen
Poems from above the Hill & Selected Work by Ashur Etwebi,
      translated by Brenda Hillman and Diallah Haidar
Puppet Wardrobe by Daniel Tiffany
Quarry by Carolyn Guinzio
remanence by Boyer Rickel
Signs Following by Ger Killeen
The Flying House by Dawn-Michelle Baude
The Prison Poems by Miguel Hernández, translated by Michael Smith
The Wash by Adam Clay
These Beautiful Limits by Thomas Lisk
Under the Quick by Molly Bendall
Verge by Morgan Lucas Schuldt
What Stillness Illuminated by Yermiyahu Ahron Taub
Winter Journey [Viaggio d'inverno] by Attilio Bertolucci,
      translated by Nicholas Benson

CPSIA information can be obtained at www.ICGtesting.com
Printed in the USA
BVOW041520200911

271492BV00001B/49/P